AN UNSPEAKABLE SECRET

Glenda L. Hunter

Foreword by Steve Hunter

Resource *Publications*
An imprint of *Wipf and Stock Publishers*
150 West Broadway • Eugene OR 97401

Resource *Publications*
an imprint of Wipf and Stock Publishers
150 West Broadway
Eugene, Oregon 97401

An Unspeakable Secret
By Hunter, Glenda L.

ISBN: 1-59244-042-8
Publication date: September, 2002
Previously published by NPP, 2002.

FOREWORD

One day while at work I received a call from a lady who identified herself as a therapist. She said she had been seeing my wife, Glenda, for a couple of months. It was a shock to me. I knew nothing about it. The therapist had a dilemma. She didn't know who to call, the police or me, because my wife was suicidal.

I called home. My wife denied that she knew the therapist. I let her know that I knew how she was feeling and I made her promise that she would not hurt herself. She finally said okay. I told her to stay there and I would be home in a few minutes. I remained calm as much as possible and asked some of my coworkers to pray for us. I headed home.

I arrived home, went in and found her in our bedroom. She was sitting there in the dark. I asked her how she was doing. She did not say much. I sat beside her on the floor and put my arm around her. She said she had been hurt. She did not say who it was. With the Lord's help, I knew who it was--her dad. It was then I began my journey with Glenda to reveal the unspeakable secret.

Even though this secret caught us by surprise, God was not in the dark. His plan unfolded for us in an amazing way. He had us in the right place at the right time. All the key people were here, from the right therapists to our friends and support people. I was her night therapist who held her while she cried herself to sleep and talked to her when she woke up terrified.

It was a long, hard journey with many ups and downs for Glenda to find wholeness. It was not only God's plan for Glenda to find wholeness, but there was always her motivation to get better. Countless times Glenda said she wanted to get better and find the light at the end of the tunnel. These key factors came together with God's guiding hand for her to become the person God wanted her to be for His glory, her benefit and her ministry to others. God helped us every step of the way and carried us quite often. He helped us find light at the end of this long, dark tunnel.

Steve Hunter
August 19, 2002

The names in this book have been changed to protect the privacy of the people.

DEDICATED:

To my therapists without whom there would be no book, and to the many people out there who think they are the only ones suffering from sexual abuse.

THANKS:

To my therapists who had faith in me and concern for my wholeness, which has kept me on the journey. I thank each of you for your hard work and good therapy.

A special thanks to my friend who first encouraged me to seek help and faithfully stood by me when the hard times came.

My dear husband deserves a special thanks, because he has been by my side encouraging me all along the way. He has been my biggest cheerleader and a very loving companion. He has stood with me in the tough times and continues to love me unconditionally. Thank you, my dear.

Last, but not the least, is God. I owe Him all. A special thank you seems very small, but He knows my heart and how big the thank you really is. I am thankful for His faithfulness, even when I was not so loving.

Thank you, God, for everything!

CONTENTS

Chapter 1

WALK, LEGS, WALK

After a very restless night, I slowly dragged my body from bed, moaning and groaning. Although it seemed as if I had just gone to sleep, the reality of the situation was that it was time to start another day. As I walked to the bathroom, I realized I definitely had a problem. My legs did not want to cooperate. The pain in my legs made me feel as if I had gained one hundred pounds overnight, and my knees were buckling under the strain of it all. Taking a closer look, I noticed my knees were swollen. It was no big deal. This had happened before. The solution had always been to keep off my feet, and my knees would get better after they were rested.

I phoned my boss and explained the situation to her. She was very understanding and recommended that I take the day off and rest. I assured her that I would be back to work on Monday. After hanging up the phone, I crawled back into bed where I spent the whole weekend. The weekend came and went, but I was not able to return to work because the swelling just got worse. The pain and the swelling made it impossible to do my regular activities.

I don’t enjoy going to the doctor, but at this point I had no option. It was a necessity. I was glad when I quickly got a doctor's appointment. My legs were so sore, I walked as if I had saddle sores from being on a horse too long. I hobbled down to the examining room, only to be told he wasn't sure what was wrong. His advice was to go to a specialist. This was not music to my ears because I was ready for instant relief.

Hobbling everywhere I went, I hobbled on over to the specialist's office. He poked around on my knees to see if they hurt. I could have told him that they did before he touched me. The pain was increasing, but nothing showed up on the x-rays. My heart sank. “What do I do now?” was my thought.

In examining my knees again, the doctor realized that the muscle holding the left knee cap in place was very small and wasn’t holding it in place as needed, causing my pain. The right knee was swollen because of the extra strain it was under. I was fitted for a brace and wore it all the time except when in bed. The brace didn’t feel good either because it was hot and the knee kept swelling.

The treatment prescribed was Advil and exercises. I wasn’t sure how this would help, but I was ready to try anything. I began my treatment and prayed for the best. I expected rapid relief, but I was only fooling myself.

The doctor said I could go back to work when I felt like it. I called my boss in a few days and was ready to work, although I still could not do my regular activities around the house. I went back to work and got very sick. I went to my boss's house and stayed until I was able to drive home. Again I had to stop working. I could hardly believe this was happening to me.

I was attending seminary, studying for full time Christian service, and here I was able to do very little. I went to classes, but it became increasingly difficult. Sitting put a strain on my knees. As a class session continued, I became a "watch watcher," hoping the class would soon end. The pain would become so great that I would become sick to my stomach and looked for every opportunity to walk or stretch my legs out on a chair.

I tried hard not to let people know how much pain I was in. I would often come home and cry. I was unable to do any walking that was not an absolute necessity. Elevating my legs made the pain tolerable. I finally got tired of suffering in class and explained my problem to the professors. They were very understanding, and told me if it would help to put my legs up, then elevate them. I began to do just that. This enabled me to continue my classes. It was a great help after I stretched my legs onto the chair in front of me. I continued going to school, but was unable to go back to work.

Doing things around the house was another story. By the time I went to school, I had no energy left to do anything. Besides being exhausted, I could not stand up. even with the brace on my knee. Fixing meals was a challenge. I began to teach my two boys how to fix things. I would sit on the couch giving directions, and when needed, I would hobble to the kitchen to help them. We ate a lot of pizza, but no one complained. Everyone was willing to help share the burden.

During these days of rest, my mind became very active. I wondered what God was trying to teach me. It would not be the first time He had to slow me down so I could hear Him. Lying on the couch or bed, I listened very carefully for His voice. I did not find any great revelation, but I kept searching for His will. I was very thankful that He gave me the ability to do my studies, because it was very hard to concentrate.

To my sorrow, I began to remember things about my childhood. They were very negative things. Years before I had asked God to take these things from my memory, because I had already asked for forgiveness. They would leave for a while and then return to haunt me. I hadn't thought about these things for a very long time. I thought they were gone forever, but they were back. I couldn't share this with anyone because I was too ashamed.

I had been talking to my dear friend, Gloria, who recommended that I go to a counselor. I hadn't shared my deep shame with her, but she was wise enough to know I needed professional help.

It was hard for me to admit that I needed help, but when I became convinced, I called a nearby seminary that had a counseling program. I picked up the phone and slowly dialed the number. As the phone rang the first time, I hoped that there would be no answer and I could at least say I tried. When someone answered on the second ring, I could hardly talk. My name even left me.

Looking up from the phone, I caught a glimpse of Gloria, and I knew I had to continue. Taking a deep breath, I was able to blurt out my name and that I wanted to see a counselor. The lady on the other end sounded very kind and said she would put my name on a list. I gave her Gloria's phone number, because I did not want my husband to know. I felt it was my problem and I would take care of the situation.

Now, I had to wait.

I am not a very patient person, but I began my wait. The hours became days and the days became weeks, but no call came. I had buried myself in my studies and was finally able to return to work. It was hard to concentrate on my studies when my mind was so busy with other things. I was beginning to feel a sense of relief that the seminary had forgotten my case and I was no longer on the list. I had been praying that if God wanted me to get this kind of help they would call. I had convinced myself that this was not what God had for me to do. I am a Christian; God and I will be able to deal with whatever by ourselves. There should be no need for any outside help. My heart was feeling a little lighter, and I even felt happy because I was very relieved.

After arriving at Gloria's house one day for a visit, the phone rang. To my surprise, it was for me. On the other end was a Mrs. Smith, a counselor, and she wanted to set up an appointment with me. I stuttered around and finally made an appointment. We were going to meet the following week at her house. She gave me directions to her house. I could hardly remember the street she lived on, let alone the directions on how to get there.

I was in shock. I hung up the phone and could hardly talk, because I was sure they had forgotten me. When I came to myself, I began to tell Gloria about the phone call. I also shared with her my previous conversation with God. Gloria just laughed, because she had been talking to God about my concern. She said she had asked God to have someone call me or she was going to call the seminary and see where I was on the list. I felt sure then that this was what God wanted me to do. I was really concerned how this would look for me--a Christian having to go to a counselor? What would people say? I knew I shouldn't worry about that, but I did. I didn't tell anyone but Gloria. She had promised not to tell anyone, so I would be safe. The rest of the week was filled with great anxiety.

When I arrived for my appointment, I was greeted by Mrs. Smith, who showed me to her office. I felt like I was ready to spill everything, but when she asked me what I wanted to talk about, I was left speechless. Talking to someone about my family was not easy. Even talking about my own shortcomings was very difficult. She sat there ready to listen, but I couldn't find the words to speak.

Finally I was able to say, "Let me tell you a little about myself." I began to tell her the size of my family, where I came in the line of children, and how I was made to feel. After talking for only a little while, it was time to leave. I thought I would not be coming many times so I had to make every minute count, and I felt that I had not accomplished very much. But Mrs. Smith was very encouraging and said I did very well. As I was leaving, she said she would see me again next week at the same time. That was not what I wanted to hear, but I decided I would return for one more session.

I returned as scheduled. When I went back to the office, I found it extremely hard to sit still. After just a little while, I was up and walking around. Although there was not much room, it was better then sitting. After pacing back and forth, I began to spill my dark secret. My thinking was, "I'll tell this, then I'll be able to forget it once and for all and get on with life." But I was in for a surprise.

The story I began to reveal was that when I was a little girl, my older brother used to touch me in a very improper way. When this first began to happen, I didn't think much about it, even though I did not enjoy the touching at all. When I asked him to stop, he paid no attention. He threatened to tell Mom and then I would be in big trouble. I knew Mom would probably be on his side and I would be in trouble, but I was tired of the whole situation. I told him to go ahead and tell Mom. He didn't tell her, and it was over for the time--but not forgotten. As I got a little older and began to develop, things began to happen again.

I enjoyed playing all sports, but it began to be a fight for my privacy. When we played football and basketball, he would make it a point to grab my breast and squeeze as hard as he could. I didn't like to be touched, let alone grabbed. Touching must have been a thing for my brother, but I did not want to be his touchy toy. I felt like I was a dirty person.

I was fed up with the grabbing and stopped playing football, but I loved playing basketball so much I decided to fight. Whenever he would grab me unnecessarily, I would hit him and knock him down. He would complain to Mom, and she would tell me to be more careful. But when he hit me and knocked me around, mom would say, "if you can't take it, you shouldn't play." I became a roughneck. After a while it all seemed to subside, but to my sad sorrow, things were not over.

When I was about fifteen, I stayed at another brother's house to watch their children while they went out of state to a funeral. My abusive brother was also staying there because he had to work. Things were going along smoothly until one night when we were watching a beauty pageant. All of a sudden he turned to me and said, "Let me see your figure." Being very sly, I stood up and said, "There. This is it." This was not what he meant.

Later I found out what he really was after. I got tired of watching the pageant and went to get a bath before bed. I had locked the door and intended on having a nice leisurely bath, but I was interrupted when

I heard the door unlock. My brother had fixed the door so it could be unlocked from the outside. In the past the children had locked themselves in, so the parents now had this safety measure. My brother was planning to come in because he wanted to see my figure with my clothes off.

I was really angry and told him if he came in I would kill him. He stopped and didn't enter, but he sure put a scare in me. I don't think I would have killed him, but I think I would have killed myself. I felt that I must have asked for all of this in some way. There were other times during that stay that my brother would be looking over me when I woke up. I never rested very well, because I was never sure what he would do.

There I had spilled my horrible secret. Now, I waited for a response.

I was ready to hear how awful I was, but I was surprised that was not what I heard. Instead, I heard that I had every right to be angry. Mrs. Smith seemed to understand the rage that came out as my story was revealed.

I was ready for a quick fix, but quick fixes were not in her treatment. I was hoping she would tell me something that would relieve the guilt, so that my life would return to normal. I had already told God all about the situation, but I was still greatly troubled. Maybe now things would be different.

Her suggestion of more sessions to help me work through the trauma this had caused was not my idea of a good time. I decided I would take some drastic measures and talk about finances. I thought this would be foolproof, so there would be no more sessions and she would give me a quick fix. When I explained to her that I only had enough money for the two completed sessions, she was very gracious. I was shocked almost out of my shoes when she said she was willing to work with me anyway. The plan was, whenever I had the money I would pay and when I didn't have it, that was also okay. She wanted me to continue to come. What could I say to such an offer? Of course, I continued to go. God had worked out all the details.

I gave myself a full month. I figured I could have all the problems of my past and any present ones taken care of in that time. I knew I wasn't in that bad of shape. Besides, I was not worth her taking any more time with me. I was sure by that time she would be very tired of the whole business.

The issues of my childhood became deeper and deeper. My thinking began to be cloudy. My prayers even had to be written. As I've read back over them, I have found out they were prayers of thanksgiving to God for helping me. Also I would thank Him for making me, even though there were times I didn't like who I was. He had made me a worthwhile person, and I would ask Him to keep reminding me of that fact. But nothing seemed to relieve me of the awful, guilty feeling I had deep inside.

Here is more of my childhood story. When I was six I began to attend Sunday School. It was there I heard about Jesus. I remember my teachers telling me that Jesus loved me, and that some day I could go and live with Him if I followed Him. I didn't understand all of this, but I held onto the fact that Jesus loved me. My deep desire was to go live with Him.

That didn't help the turmoil that boiled inside now. I knew what happened was wrong, and I carried all the blame. I began to wonder for the first time if God could even love me.

The actions of my brother bothered me more then I wanted anyone to know. I felt very helpless in the situation, even though I was a tomboy and very much a fighter. I was sure this was not pleasing to God, but in my child's mind I didn't know what else to do. It seemed that fighting was my only escape from the torture I felt.

The pain seemed overwhelming as I continued to visit Mrs. Smith and we talked about my childhood. Sometimes I would laugh at things that were very painful; it was my way of not facing the pain. I didn't enjoy talking about my childhood, but found it very necessary. There had been many things said to me that caused deep scars that have affected my whole life. The more we talked, the more uneasy I became.

While I sat on the couch, I would pick up Mrs. Smith's teddy bear and hold it like a small child. It held a bit of comfort. Another way of handling the situation was to run. When things got heavy, I was ready to leave her office--no need to talk anymore; just let me out of here. I would be up and headed for the door. Mrs. Smith was very wise and began to know how to channel me back into facing the real situation. I know God guided her in her efforts.

On one particular visit, something memorable occurred. I was sitting on the couch holding the teddy bear as usual, but feeling very frightened. The little girl inside was in such pain and fear. I was looking for a safe place for her to stay. The little girl was in great pain and fear possessed her. As I was holding the teddy bear that day, I "left" the little girl there to be cared for. I knew Mrs. Smith was a caring person who could give the little girl the love she needed. Slowly and carefully, I placed the teddy bear on the couch. Not telling Mrs. Smith what I had done, I prepared to leave. As I left, I had an empty feeling inside, but I also felt pleased that I found a safe place for the child to stay.

As I drove to Wal-Mart it was as if the little girl was right by my side saying, "Why did you reject me? Why did you kick me out? You are like the rest of the people. No one cares for me."

Shocked, I was at a loss for words. When I came to myself, I tried to explain to her that Mrs. Smith could take very good care of her, and I was not sure I could handle her pain. But she didn't want to hear.

"I wasn't rejecting you, but I wanted us both to be able to rest," I said in my efforts to convince her of my good heart. This did not satisfy her, but she left.

When I arrived at the store, I could hardly function. There was not a smile to be found and laughing was impossible. It was the worst. I couldn't make it without the little girl. She was more important than I would have ever realized.

Arriving at home, I knew I needed the little girl, but I was afraid if I told my counselor she would think I had lost all my senses. I reached for the phone a number of times to call her and ask her to send the little girl home to me. I was afraid--mostly that something would happen to the little girl because she was so little. It would be unsafe for her to come by herself.

All of these things ran through my mind as I dialed Mrs. Smith's number. The phone rang. I was still uncertain what I was going to say. When Mrs. Smith answered the phone in her loving way, I began to stutter, not really sure what to say. I hung up the phone without sharing with her why I really called. I sat on my bed feeling very lost and alone, but I was sure I could handle the situation.

The next day as I was coming home from the seminary, I was extremely disappointed and unsure what to do. Feeling I could not go on any longer, I saw a truck coming and wanted to pull out in front of it. As I looked to check the speed of the car, I picked the speed, sure that I could pull out in front of the truck without any problem. But the steering wheel wouldn't move, and I was left in my own lane.

I wasn't happy feeling like I couldn't even kill myself right. I was really screwed up. Next, I saw God's protecting hand upon me, even in my time of uncertainty. My circuits were overloaded. I tried to escape by sleeping, but that didn't work. There was no escape.

In a couple of days I was in a state of panic. I had promised my counselor I would call her if things got too bad. As the phone rang to my counselor's house, I was hoping that she was not there. Just then, she answered the phone. I let her know that things were really bad and that I was unsure what to do.

When we were getting ready to hang up, she asked me to promise I would not hurt myself. I wouldn't make that promise. I didn't know what I was going to do, but I was planning something. She began to panic and wanted to come over, but I wouldn't tell her where I lived.

I wasn't really thinking of how mean that might seem. I just wanted to put a stop to the pain. Knowing she was not only a lady of prayer, but of action as well, I figured I had to put a stop to anything she might do. She continued to talk to me and asked me where my husband worked, and without thinking I told her. Then shortly we hung up. I felt very proud of myself because I felt I had control of the situation. I was not giving her enough credit.

Soon the phone began to ring. Slowly I reached to answer, picked up the receiver, and as pleasantly as possible, I said, "Hello."

"Hello, Glenda, how are you?" My husband's voice came across the telephone wires. Mrs. Smith had called him. Now it was my job to convince him that she was over-reacting. I told him I was doing fine, but he wasn't buying it.

"I just got off the phone with Mrs. Smith. I think you know her," was his serious reply.

"Oh, who could that be?" I asked, trying to sound puzzled.

"I'm coming home so we can talk," he said with great concern.

What could I say to help calm him down? I was kind of embarrassed, but kind of relieved that he finally knew. It had been a hard secret to hide.

That day began to change a lot of things for us. . His coming home showed me that he really cared. He seemed to know my thoughts and had me promise that I would not hurt myself, so he could return to work. I promised, and he returned to finish his job. He was very supportive, but this was *my* problem, and I didn't want to involve him. I was going to work through this by myself.

I questioned whether my counselor would even want to see me anymore. Even as I arrived for my next meeting, I was still very uncertain. Walking in her house and back to her office, I waited for her to tell me to leave because she did not want to see me anymore. I sat down on the couch and waited for the bomb. There was no bomb; no telling me how stupid I was. She didn't throw me out. She was very gracious and still wanted to work with me. Talk about being shocked; that was my state of mind at this point.

I was finally able to get my little girl back! I picked up the teddy bear to retrieve her. It was a relief to have her back. I explained to Mrs. Smith the whole situation about leaving the little girl. She told me she would have understood if only I would have told her. She said I could have come by and picked her up. It was good to have her back, even though I still hurt.

Other things began to come up. My counselor was very patient and would listen with her heart, as well as her ears. One of the things I shared was how I hated to be called "stupid." I had heard this word all the time when I was growing up. It never mattered what I did, I was always considered stupid. This had haunted me all my life. Even though I was working on a Master's degree, I still had a hard time believing that I wasn't stupid. And though there were times I'm sure I didn't make any sense to my counselor, not once did she call me stupid. She continued to gain my respect and confidence.

Another feeling that overwhelmed me was one of worthlessness. If someone spent very much time helping me, then I felt they wanted something from me. I was in no shape to give much to anyone. I felt that Mrs. Smith was wasting her time because there was certainly someone more important that she could be helping...something more important that she could be doing.

In my mind, I was saying, "I'm sure you don't want me around because you have more important things to do. You can kick me out any time. t will be no problem; I understand."

Mrs. Smith would continue to assure me I was not bothering her. She even said she enjoyed working with me. This was really a new concept--someone enjoys working with me! I would have to think about that one for awhile.

My sessions were very stressful and I found one thing I always wanted to do was run. When things began to hit too close to home and I didn't want to deal with them, I told her it was time I leave. It seemed I was leaving more than I was coming. Sometimes the desire to run came at the beginning of my session. In her sweet, patient way she would convince me to stay. She knew if I could stand and face whatever the problem, I would be farther along. I tried to do just that, even though it was not easy.

This desire to run was not just a characteristic of that part of therapy; it was carried throughout all of my therapy. I didn’t know how else to handle the pressure.

After awhile I began to dissociate, which was as close to running as I could get without leaving the room.

Running was never really an answer because memories were with me wherever I went. There was no escape. I also tried to cover things up. It's called denial, but that never worked either. Facing things was the only solution.

I had also become very angry with God. "Where are You? Why are You not helping? How could You let this happen?" These questions haunted me for a long time as I tried to search for an answer. At the same time, I was afraid to admit this to anyone, because of the kind of person I was becoming. I wanted to be known as a good Christian, and how could I be with this attitude? I thought that if I admitted this anger, He would leave me. To me, that thought was worse than death.

I would like to share a part of a prayer with you:

Dear God,

If You were here right now physically, I would take hold of You and shake You. As I shake You, I would be yelling, "Why didn't You protect me when I was a kid? Why did You allow me to be hurt so badly? Was I such a bad kid that You saw no need to take care of a failure like me? You know I tried to be good, but I just wasn't good enough."

You can see that I was quite upset and wondering about everything. "Do ye fear the weakness within thine own self? Lo, I have put it there to drive thee to Myself. I may never answer thy prayers to be made strong, but I will give you the same promise I gave Paul, that in your weakness I will be your strength. For it is still true that My grace operates most effectively when ye have a conscious sense of need--yea, even a desperate awareness of your own complete helpless-ness."[1]

Although the feelings of weakness and helplessness were very great, my mind never stopped to gather things together before I began to remember things in a dream. One dream I had about my dad was very disturbing: We were in court and my dad was on trial for molesting little girls. I was very shocked and sure there was a mistake. My dad was a quiet man and never bothered anyone. The girls were now grown. But they felt that they needed to tell what had happened because they didn't want it to happen to anyone else. These ladies began to scream for me to tell what had happened to me.

I was shocked because nothing had happened to me--or I couldn't remember anything. But this didn't stop their yelling, "Tell! Tell!" It was like a flood of voices

---

[1]Frances J. Roberts, Come Away My Beloved (Ojai: Kings Farspan, Inc., 1970), p. 115.

running into my ears, and I had to cover my ears so my eardrums would not burst.

"I know nothing, I know nothing," I kept screaming while they continued to yell, "Tell what happened before you were five."

I felt a bit relieved because I remembered nothing before I was six; I was finally off the hook. Everyone seemed to know something I did not know. They wouldn't let it rest. They kept insisting I knew. I became really frightened as I looked into Dad's face and saw his anger. I was sure it was better that I not know.

I was haunted by the dream. Then I began to remember--a little at a time--how my father had sexually abused me when I was a small child. I felt like I was going crazy. My mind began to race. Sexual abuse in my family? no way!

I was immediately filled with denial, and soon found it would be something that I would continue to have to deal with. I must really be dreaming now; surely it is just a case of an overactive imagination. Denying the truth is much easier than facing the truth when it is so traumatic, but I knew I must deal with the facts in order to continue my journey to wholeness.

Chapter 2

WOW! WHAT A SECRET

As I lay there in bed enjoying my husband's tender touch all of a sudden I began to become someone else. My upper arms hurt from the pressure I felt, although nothing was there to make such a feeling. It was very real. Then my eyes began to swell with tears. I began to cry softly.

"What's the matter with me?," my husband wanted to know, as he tried to put his arms around me. There was no way I wanted him to touch me, let alone put his arms around me. I was very frightened, just wanting the pain to stop.

As I lay there in a state of shock, I began to tell the most unbelievable story. My husband said I sounded like I was three years old as I told my story. I begged him to stop the hurting as I talked. I had started to have memories of my childhood abuse. The pain I was having was a body memory of what it really felt like those many years ago. My husband listened with a very loving heart and a sympathetic ear.

The little child that told the story was very much afraid of everyone. My arms ached because my dad would put his big legs on my little arms holding me down while he abused me. The pain was so great in my arms I felt sure he was doing it again. This was the beginning of what would be a long and hard time of memory of both body and mind.

The next few days were some of high anxiety and little sleep. Going to see Mrs. Smith was going to be a welcome relief, I hoped, but it was very hard. I felt I should tell her what had happened, but then what would she think of me?

After awhile I sat on the floor and began to tell her what had happened. She never thought any less of me, and she still was willing to see me. I was sure after she knew this that she would not want to see me anymore. She was very sympathetic and ready to comfort, but I did not want her to hug me, because when I was that little no one hugged me—that I remembered anyway—except in an abusive way. She thought this needed to be explored more, but I was just glad to have it over. I thought once I told her that would be all that was necessary. I didn't give very many details because I felt that was not important.

I remembered more as time went on, and it was equally unpleasant. Slowly crawling upon dad's lap, I was looking for the same thing other toddlers do--cuddling, hugging, kissing, and all around loving. But I was to receive more then I bargained for. As I proudly sat there on Dad's lap, he put his fingers in my panties.

I wasn't aware this was bad; it had to be okay because it was my dad. At the age of one-and-a-half or two, a child doesn't know bad from good unless taught by their parents or guardian. A child believes Mom and Dad even if they are wrong because the child cannot reason yet.

I was one of four pre-school children in the family. My mom had her hands full as she tried to get each of us ready in the morning as well as getting the school-age children ready for school. We younger children were tended to after the others went to school. I tried to be helpful, but being only three it was hard to be of much benefit. I tried to give my little brother his bottle and feed him, but he would cry and I didn't know what to do.

"Get out from under my feet. I'm trying to feed your brothers," Mom would yell at me, as I tried to help with my baby brother.

"I'm only trying to help. I really can be a big help," I said, as I tried to give my brother his bottle. But the yelling would continue even more.

Mom had a solution to her problem. She would send me into the bedroom with my dad. I was really wanting to help, but thought this was a good trade. Usually he did not spend much time with us one-on-one because there were quite a few of us. I eagerly went to the bedroom and climbed in bed with him. He hugged me, tickled me, and kissed me all over. It was really fun, and he made me laugh hard. I began to look forward to these times when I had all his attention. But the fun soon ceased.

Things were beginning to get a little strange, but I didn't realize this at the time. He would take my panties off even when I objected. He told me it was okay for Daddy to see me without my panties, so I figured it must be fine. This didn't bother me much because we were still having fun.

One day when I came in, he showed me himself, and I laughed. I had never seen anything so funny looking. He slapped me and told me to never laugh at him again. I was really sorry, but he became very angry. This is when he began to teach me a new game, one I couldn't share with anyone. This was to be our secret that no one else was to ever know.

I thought it was very exciting to have a special game just for us. He would tell me how special I was to him, how pretty my hair was, and that I was his chosen. He also told me that if I told anyone about this game they would call me a liar. I wanted to tell Mom, but he made me promise not to tell before he would teach the game to me. I was excited about a game just for us.

The excitement was soon over. My times with Dad became times of great pain, fear, and confusion. Dad did all kinds of unmentionable things to me, and I was in pain for a long time after it was over. It seemed that I lived in pain all the time. This would happen five out of seven days for weeks and longer. Fear was always gripping my body because I was never sure what was going to happen. When he became mad, he was like a monster out of control.

I was confused because I never understood what he wanted of me. One time it would be one way; the next it would be something different. Dad was quick to tell me how bad I was. No longer was I his special little girl. According to him, I was a whore and a slut. I didn't know what these words meant, but I knew it wasn't good. Somehow I had become an awful person who couldn't do anything right. I wasn't sure what had changed to make me this kind of a person.

"Mom," I would beg, "please let me stay out here with you. I will help with the boys."

"No," she would reply angrily, "go in there and stay with Dad until I get finished with the boys."

I would go slowly to the bedroom door. Opening it with great fear, I would enter. As I slowly walked in, Dad was eager for me to climb into bed. He quickly lifted me on the bed and took off my clothes. I felt like I was being thrown into the lions' den day after day. The lion would claw me very badly.

It was hard trying to satisfy him. He would become very angry and violent when things didn't go exactly the way he wanted. There were times I was not good enough. He would slap me and call me all kinds of bad names. He did not like me to cry. Whenever that would happen, he would slap me and tell me he would give me something to cry about. I learned how to hold back my tears while I was with him. I thought if he saw the tears in my eyes he would know my heart was breaking.

I tried to be good so he would be proud of me, but that didn't happen. When he was done abusing me in the morning, he would have me sit on a chair. His explanation was that I had misbehaved and needed to be punished. Mom never questioned anything he said, so there I sat in the corner. The boys would run by and laugh at me because they knew I had been bad. I could hear Dad telling them in the other room that I was a really bad girl. The only thing I wanted to do was to go outside and play. While I sat on the chair and listened to the boys, not only did my body ache, but my little heart was breaking into pieces.

One morning while Dad was having his fun at my expense, Mom came in. Quickly he laid down and put his arms around me. Mom wanted me to go get dressed, but Dad said he just wanted to hug me awhile longer.

Mom left the room and left me unguarded. As I walked out of the bedroom, there she stood. I was still hoping she would protect her little girl. My sad little eyes looked up at her in hopes she would stop my pain, but to my sad sorrow she said nothing. She just gave me a strange look that I learned to obey from across the room. I slowly walked to my room without a word. My heart was crying because Mom did not rescue me.

I began to believe that if I could only get outside I would be safe. For a while that worked, then Dad began to find me and send me to the shed. As I first went to the shed I was afraid of what would happen. I was right; he wanted to play. I began to rebel. I didn't quickly undress as he demanded. I knew I would get slapped around, but I didn't really care. He began to bring in a twig from the tree and inform me by the time he took the bark off, I'd better be undressed. He also would begin hitting me with it if I was not fast enough. I slowly did what I was told, but I knew it was not right. Now I was five years old and tired of the pain that I suffered.

One day when he came in the shed I decided, "No more." He had a large twig. Slowly he peeled it as I clutched my clothes. I was not taking them off this time, no matter what happened. He became very angry and began to hit me with the twig. Harder and harder came the blows. I knew if my clothes got torn, Mom would be really mad, but I figured that was the only way he was getting them off.

He kept hitting me very hard on my back, and it began to ache. He was also yelling at me. I was very frightened, but still determined not to give in. I knew he could kill me very easily if he chose to. Instead he only beat me. Since this was not the first time, it was no big deal to me. The stick kept striking my back time and time again. I was beginning to question if I would die, but it was okay because I wouldn't have to suffer any longer.

He finally stopped. Tears filled my eyes but none rolled down my cheeks. Before he left the shed, he informed me that he never wanted to see me again. When he left, I curled up in the corner, holding my legs close to me, afraid to move. After some time, Mom called because it was time for supper. I went in and, with a sick feeling in my stomach, I told her I was too sick to eat. Off to my room I went in hopes no one would say anything. Crawling into bed, I pulled the covers snug around my neck. When Mom poked her head in the door after supper, I pretended to be asleep. As with many nights before, it would be a sleepless night with tears softly falling on my pillow.

Even as I remembered these days, the body memories were very real; my back would hurt so badly I couldn't even lay on it. It was as if the pain were happening at that very moment.

My family was preparing to move shortly after this incident, but I wasn't sure if I was going with them. My mind was racing, trying to figure out how I could not see Dad anymore and still live in the same house. As things were being packed, I kept an eye on my things so I could figure out what was going to be done with me. Finally, my things were packed along with everyone else's. But I was not relaxed yet, because I was still not sure I would be found among the children crammed into the car. At last I was among the others. What a relief.

But Dad really meant he didn't want to see me anymore. After those days, he treated me as if I never existed. I became a nobody until one day when he decided he wanted to abuse me again. It seemed that he was never satisfied. Then he would revert to the same pattern of pretending I was not even around. So in all reality, I had lost my father. I saw him every day. I still wanted him to be pleased with me, but there was no way. It didn't matter what I did or how hard I tried to please him; it just was not to be.

Psalm 27:10 says, "When my father and mother forsake me, Then the Lord will take care of me." [*New*

King James Version) Did anyone understand the hurt I felt deep inside? The little girl hurt very much, but did anyone care? My mind was racing with remembering and re-living these events, wondering where help was to be found.

During this time I wrote a little poem to God:

I HURT INSIDE

O God, Do You know how I hurt?
Do You care that my heart breaks?
I am just a little girl, one that likes to run and play.
I like having lots of fun.
But I became a sad, quiet little girl when Dad began
to abuse
me.
I was being hurt but no one seemed to care.
I do not know how to tell big people what is going
on.
But I am afraid they would not believe
whatever I
said.
My tears are many but they flow on the inside.
I try very hard not to let them slip down my
face.
Because when my Dad sees these horrible tears,
he slaps me
and becomes very angry.
I am just little, but I know what is happening is
wrong.
Will this ever end or will I always be afraid?
I often cry and scream on the inside for someone to
help or
care.
But the people walking by have no idea of
the hurt

that lies deep inside.
God, do You know what is happening?
I hear You are very loving, and that You care for
children.
I am not sure how You care for us but I am glad
You do.
God, I do have a big favor to ask of You.
Will you please put Your arms around me and hold
me close?
I need someone to take care of me.
I need to be able to rest without fear.
Thank You for caring.
Cindy
[one of my alters])

All of this remembering was causing a very serious problem. I was becoming "a basket case." Life was no fun. It was becoming unbearable. I had to drop out of seminary and stop working. Coping was about all I could do, and even that wasn't very well done. Mrs. Smith was working hard with me, but I was in big time denial. I remembered Dad as a quiet, firm man--not as someone who did monstrous things.

I listened to music all the time so I wouldn't think, and I began to find songs that expressed how I felt. One of those songs was written by Joni Eareckson Tada. It described how I felt about my life.

When Special Things Get Broken

I have a piece of china; a pretty porcelain vase.
It holds such lovely flowers, captures everybody's gaze.
But fragile things just slip and fall, as everybody knows,
and when my vase came crashing down
those tears began to flow.

[CHORUS[*Don't we all cry when pretty things get broken?*
Don't we all sigh at such an awful loss?
Jesus will dry your tears as He has spoken,
'cause He was the one broken on the cross.

My life was just like china--a lovely thing to me,
full of porcelain promises of all that I might be.
But fragile things just slip and fall, as everybody knows,
and when my life came crashing down
those tears began to flow.

Now Jesus is no porcelain prince,.
His promises won't break.
His Holy Word has spots unsure,
His love no one can shake.
So if your life is shattered by sorrow, pain or sin,
His healing love will reach right down
and make you whole again.

There were also other things I did to try to come to grips with my life. One of the things I did was walk. I was always seeking answers to my many questions, and this was no different. One day as I walked, I became very frustrated. It seemed that in my questioning mind, I was getting nowhere.

Bending down, I would pick up some rocks so I could throw them in hopes of releasing some tension. I actually felt that my head was going to pop because it hurt so bad. I began to throw, but the great release I anticipated did not come. Stopping before I threw the last rock, I just tossed it in the air and caught it time and again. Then I began to just hold it, and from the small rock I learned an important lesson.

It was quite an ordinary rock. One side was smooth and pretty; the other side was rough and really ugly. As I carried this rock, I rubbed the blemished side trying to make the blemishes disappear, but they were there to stay. I began to compare the rock to my own life and the blemishes I had discovered that made it appear ugly. It was impossible to throw the rock away, because I felt like it would be saying it was okay to throw my life away. I realized I really didn't want to do that. Just because the rock was not perfect did not mean it was worthless. It was as if the Lord was saying to me, "You are only blemished, but still you are of value."

Carrying the rock with care, I wanted to protect the more vulnerable spots. I put the rock in my pocket and carried it with me everywhere. When I went to see Mrs. Smith it was still in my pocket. Pulling it out, I handed it to her as I told the story.

To my surprise when I was done, she said that she held the rock as if to protect the roughness. I carried it in my pocket for awhile after that, but could never come to throw it away. Finally, I gave the rock to

Mrs. Smith. That was my sign that I was accepting my own situation a little more. I knew God was showing me that He was my protector.

All my life I had never really experienced feelings like some other people, because I had always been told not to feel this way or that. All of this remembering brought up a number of feelings. Shame was one of those dreaded emotions. Webster says "shame" is something that brings strong regret.

I've always felt that if people knew me they would not like me. These memories magnified that feeling. I was ashamed of who I was. At that time I was certain since I had done these awful things, no one would like me. I could hardly look at myself in the mirror because all I could see was the awfulness of my past. The regret was so great at times that I would rather kill myself than let anyone know the real me. Even though the abuse was not my fault, I still felt the awful shame.

I also felt very dirty. At first I never realized I possessed such feelings, but my husband began to notice that my shower water was very hot. Whenever I got done with my shower, I would be really red, but it never registered to me that anything was wrong. It was a subconscious thing, but after it was brought to my attention I began to take note. I not only was turning the water on hot, but I also was scrubbing my body very hard. I guess I was trying to get rid of a couple layers of skin--maybe a couple of layers down I would be clean. It didn't matter how hot the water was or how hard I scrubbed, I could not get clean. My heart cried out, "You have been living a lie. You are not pure. You are filthy."

With great sadness, I felt the only wholesome thing to do was let my husband of twelve years be free to go. Then he could get a person deserving of his great love. My husband didnt share these feelings, but I felt I needed to give him this option. I can proudly report my husband has stayed with me, and we are continuing to grow in our love for each other.

Another feeling that overwhelmed me was guilt. "I'm guilty. I'm guilty," a voice kept screaming in my head. I was sure I had done something to make my dad act so bizarre. Certainly he would not do this on his own--he was too good a man.

"It's hard to acknowledge that you have been abused as a child because in doing so, you also admit that your parents were wrong, or not perfect. Honor thy mother and father is a very strong lesson, and seeing your parents as abusive may feel like a betrayal of them."[2]

---

[2]Eliana Gil, Outgrowing the Pain (New York: Dell Publishing, 1983), p. 14.

I had become my own judge and jury, sentencing myself to a life of unhappiness and punishment. For being such a person, I felt it would be necessary to leave my husband, children, family, and friends and go to parts unknown to live alone. I was afraid I would cause someone to act toward me as my father had. This might sound like a harsh measure, separating myself from others, but to me it was not harsh enough because of my guilt.

One night when I went to bed feeling very guilty and troubled, I had a very remarkable dream. No, I am not Joseph the dreamer, but I think we sometimes have dreams to help us see things more clearly--or even to give us an answer to a problem.

This was my dream: I was in a courtroom full of people. On one side were my husband, Mrs. Smith, and Gloria. On the other side were Dad, Mom, brothers, sisters, relatives and friends of the family. Dad had a very good lawyer; I sat at the table by myself. I was just a small child and was very frightened. People began to scream and say this was all unnecessary and that I was crazy. Fear grew within me because Dad kept giving me the look of anger--the look he would give me just before slapping me around. I was sure he would come after me.

It was time for the judge to enter. We stood up and he entered. People on the other side began to talk all at the same time. No one could be understood, but you knew the subject was had Dad really sexually abused me. This made them mad. The judge told them he had heard enough. He wanted me to speak. I was so frightened I could not form any words with my mouth. Noticing my fear, he called me to his chambers. I hadn't looked up at him this whole time, but I slowly crawled down from my chair and went to his chambers. I hesitated in the doorway and he called for me to come all the way in. I slowly entered. He sat very tall in his seat and I stayed as far away as possible. I was unaware of what to expect.

Trying to help me feel relaxed, he offered me a doll to play with, but I sadly told him I did not play with dolls. He said he would give me anything I wanted to play with. With little thought, I chose blocks. I sat on the floor and began to build, then I knocked them over. I was done playing. I just sat there, very frightened.

"Do you want someone to come in with you?" he asked with concern in his voice.

"I would like Mrs. Smith to come in," was my quick answer. As she was ushered in, I hurried to her side. Then the judge asked if I wanted to go outside. I certainly did, because I liked being where I could run and play.

As we walked out the door, I realized my judge was Jesus. This didn't make me happy because I was not sure of Him either. We walked right onto the prettiest green grass I'd ever laid eyes on. In the distance was a shade tree and to the left was a stream of the clearest blue water. It was beautiful. I began to run and have a good time. After running awhile, Mrs. Smith had to sit down and rest, but Judge Jesus never got tired. We had run for a very long time before I had finally run enough. I walked over and took hold of His hand and we began to walk, not saying a word. I decided it was time to sit down, and He joined me.

He again asked me if I could tell Him what had happened, why I was afraid of my dad. I asked if I could sit on His lap. He smiled and shook His head "Yes." He seemed pleased as I climbed up on His lap. After sitting there awhile, I began to tell the whole story. He wasn't angry; He even believed me. I was very surprised. He didn't make me go back into the courtroom.

The dream ended with His holding me, but I had received no answer. I was still left with the question: Did He think I was guilty or not?

Days passed. I was haunted because there seemed to be no answer to be found. I was beginning to think my decision was the correct one--I had judged myself guilty. After talking to Mrs. Smith, she assured me I was not guilty. I was still not satisfied. I wanted to know what Judge Jesus thought.

"Lord what is Your verdict?" I began to ask, after a number of days had passed.

Finally the answer came! "Not guilty," Judge Jesus seemed to say. Psalm 7:11 says: “God is a just judge, and God is angry with the wicked every day.” [*New King James Version*)

Another feeling that possessed me was fear. It gripped me big time. Remembering all of this unpleasantness left me feeling unsafe no matter where I was. I knew Dad would come and get me because I had told THE secret. In reality, I knew he couldn't come, because he was dead. But my fear was so great that it was hard to be realistic.

Going to bed was like a trip to the twilight zone; I was never sure just what would happen during this time. Some days I spent most of my time in bed, afraid to get up and face the day. I was constantly in search of a safe place. Finally I found a corner that seemed to be relatively safe.

Going to the store was a real challenge. There were times I felt confident everyone was out to get me. There was no place to hide, and believe me, I searched. Fear was my companion for a long time. It wouldn’t go away easily.

Anger was another emotion I had to face. I didn't want to deal with my anger. As a matter of fact, I didn't want to believe I even had such an emotion. When I felt myself getting out of control, I worked hard at not letting it surface. More will be said about this in another chapter.

Mrs. Smith began to ask me if I had forgiven my dad. I thought that was a bizarre thing to ask. Of course I hadn't. He was wrong; he needs to pay for what he did. I resented the fact that I had to pay for his sin. What I was hearing was: "Don't blame him; you take the blame. Put the situation in the past where it belongs, and go on."

According to Webster, "forgiveness" ceasing to feel resentment against someone. I realized this was something to which I would have to give a lot of thought. At this stage, I wasn't willing to forgive myself, let alone my dad.

Never oncc did Mrs. Smith say the perpetrator was in the right. In fact, she said it didn't matter how many times it had happened--even once is too many. It isn't right at any time. But my ears could not hear those words; they only heard that I was wrong and I was to forgive poor Dad.

What did it matter if I forgave him? He was dead, so no big deal. I left it like that and struggled with my other feelings for the moment.

I am inserting an illustration of how I felt inside: A battle was being fought. As in many battles, there was an innocent victim injured. After trying to mend her own wounds, the victim went to a nurse.

"Nurse, will you help me?" cried the poor wounded victim.

"Yes I will protect you," replied the kind-hearted nurse. A Band-Aid was put on the broken arm and medicine on the broken leg. But the victim continued to cry for help. The Band-Aid didn't set the arm nor the medicine heal the leg correctly. For years the hurt was still there and healing did not take place. The problem was only covered up.

The nurse did what she promised and protected the victim the best she could. The victim kept crying and screaming for help. The nurse kept telling her to be quiet and all would be well. The poor little victim hurt so much that rest was very hard to come by. The days were short and the nights were long. She began to cry out day and night, "Please, please, please help me. The hurt is more than I can bear."

The nurse didn't want her to cry any longer, but she didn't know what to do. In time, the nurse learned how to fix the wounds properly and set the broken arm and leg. Not knowing what else to do, the nurse picked the victim up and held her. Holding her ever so closely, she sat down in the rocking chair and began to rock.

In the distance, you could hear the nurse telling the little one how she loved and cared for her. The little one just smiled and rested as she had never rested before. The wounds began to heal and, as time passed, the little one became totally healed. The nurse was thrilled to have helped such a precious person.

Being a victim of an awful battle doesn't need to be fatal. Seeking the help needed and working at getting every area taken care of will benefit the healing of all victims.

Chapter 3

MANY PEOPLE DWELLING

There are a variety of ways to deal with trauma, such as developing an eating disorder, apermissive life style, schizophrenia, and multiple personality disorder (MPD]--to name just a few. MPD is developing other personalities to help care for the host. This is a very creative way of dealing with trauma.

When the trauma of sexual abuse came into my life, I learned to seek other help. I couldn't turn to my mother because I felt she knew and just didn't care or felt she could do nothing. I also didn't feel that I could turn to brothers, sisters, teachers, pastor, or even a friend. The secret must be kept. So I created my own helpers; they would come whenever things got too hard for me to handle.

Things had gotten very hard in therapy, and I was just not able to move any farther. Upon Mrs. Smith's recommendation, I got another therapist as well as her. Janet was my next therapist. She was very different from Mrs. Smith, and it took awhile to settle into her style. Now I was seeing a therapist three times a week. It seemed that I almost lived there.

After a few sessions with Janet, she told me I had MPD. I wasn't surprised, because a few months before on television I watched a program on MPD and all the facts seemed to point to me.

Okay, I have this problem; now what do I do? How can I quickly get over it? Will this be something I will always have to deal with? Should I not tell anyone? If I do, will they be afraid of me? These questions raced through my mind.

My biggest concern was the time element. How long would this take? I was always in a hurry. When Janet said at least three to five years, I felt like there was no hope. That was way too long to deal with such a simple problem.

MPD is not something to fear. You cannot catch it even if you try. "MPD is not a disease. It results from dissociation, a God-given coping style that gifted children learn to use to protect themselves from the effects of serious traumas. There is nothing wrong with these people. In fact, there is something right with them. They are talented enough to use that coping style."[3] I have always thought of myself as not being very smart, but according to what I have read and what Janet has said MPDs are smart people. If they weren't smart, they wouldn"t be able to cope in this manner.

---

[3]James G. Friesen, Ph. D., More Than Survivors Conversations With Multiple-Personality Clients (San Bernardino: Here's Life Publishers, Inc., 1992), p. 13.

You might ask why Janet called me MPD. I asked the same question. She could interpret from my words that I was coping with MPD. Of course, I wasn't aware of what I was showing her. I had lost time and could not remember what had happened. I would chalk it up to forgetfulness. My boys have even called me "Forgetful Jones." It was a big joke. I've always lost time, so it was no big concern to me.

The longer I was in therapy the worse the dissociation became. There were times I could not remember what went on in the sessions. When Janet would ask if I remembered, I would honestly say, "No I don't." I didn't recall because I wasn't really there. Janet understood this much better then I did. We would spend some time going over the same thing. It would be as if it were the first time I had ever heard it.

The real give-away was probably when I talked about others. These are alters, but I like to call them helpers since that is what they do. I was very fortunate to only need seven. They were not as well defined as some, but none the less, they were there. For example, I didn't go to my closet and find a whole new wardrobe, although sometimes that would have been nice. Also, my house was not rearranged without my knowledge. But there were times I would find myself in the toy section at the store examining all the toys. I would even be playing with them. I guess that is how kids examine them to make sure they are sturdy. Sometimes I would even go to the grocery store and only want to get snacks instead of things for meals. My boys enjoyed those times, but it didn't make my husband all that happy when it was time for supper. Sometimes I went places and wondered how I got there and why had I come. But I passed all this off as forgetfulness.

The first helper that introduced herself to me was AMBER. One day while I was very secure under my covers hoping to hibernate for the day, I was awakened by a voice I did not recognize. It was as if she was screaming at me.

"I'm Amber, I'm Amber," she said so loudly my head was ringing. I woke up and began to look around, but to my surprise I was all by myself. What a strange feeling. I covered back up and thought I must be dreaming, but the call this time was even louder than before. This time I sat up and took note. She wanted to let me know that all this abuse stuff was nonsense. That was all she had to say at the time, but she sure wanted me to know she was around.

A note from Amber to the rest: *"Listen, all of you so-called helpers. You are doing very little like everyone else in the past. I am going to take control now, and there is nothing you can do. Glenda is weak and is beginning to lack control. Therefore, I must do what she is too weak to do."*

"I am sure if I was in your office you would ask a lot of questions about me, so I thought I would tell you some things. First of all, I came at about the age of eight and have been here the rest of the time, sometimes quiet and other times not so quiet. It seems that I only come when Glenda is at her weakest, because I know that at any other time she will not listen to me. I'm no sissy or wimp. Those kinds of people just get under my skin. I 'd like to beat them up. But, oh no, Glenda says there is no reason to be so mean.

"When we were in grade school, I would be mean to the other children if they bothered me. They soon learned not to mess with me. I had to do things that way to take care of Glenda. She was very weak and got tired of all the fighting and yelling that went on in our house. It seems that I always knew what happened to her but didn't know what to do. I became the rough one ready to fight before I was even sure there was a fight."

"At the time of eight years old and older, I was the one who wanted--and still wants--her to do away with herself. For a very good reason, too! I could see her heart breaking. Why should anyone hurt like that? I never understood. But she was stronger than me, and here she still sits. I want to tell her there is a quicker way out. I will

help her. She doesn't have to go through all this pain and hurt again. I've tried to convince her to take the easy way out, but I haven't convinced her yet. She is tiring, so soon I trust she will listen to me. All these other people are doing is stringing her on. Let me help the pain to forever be gone. Think about it, Glenda. I'll be around."

Amber's job was to help keep the secret hidden and to hold Dad so high he could not be reached. She was convinced he was Mr. Perfect, and she had a hard time letting go of that idea. As certain as everyone else was of Dad's rotten, no good behavior, Amber was just as certain of his goodness. That is what she chose to believe.

The BABY was another helper, although she never actually did anything. While Glenda was in the hospital the second time, BABY came out and just cried. The tears were because of the pain, and no one would take care of her. She just needed to be hugged and comforted. She was a helpless baby with no one to care for her until all these years later. What a sad state for a baby to be in.

SALLY was your ideal child. You could call her Little Miss Princess, Miss Perfect or Miss Goody Twoshoes. When I think of Sally, I feel very proud and have a little lighter step. She was never hurt. As a matter of fact, when she would sense hurt she would go.

She thought herself to be beautiful and very smart. What a kid.

Some of my helpers didn't have names. The one I referred to as the little one wanted to be called CINDY. This came about because of a story she and I wrote. In the story the little girl had no name and was not liked by her family. After years of mistreatment, she left home so she would cause no more trouble. But a sister came to find her and thought she needed a name. The little girl always wanted to be called Cinderella. She was called Cindy for short. After Janet read the story, the little one asked if she could be called Cindy. It was agreed upon, and she was Cindy from then on.

Cindy was just the opposite of Sally; she was always getting into trouble. She was between the ages of three and five and received the bulk of the abuse: sexually, physically, emotionally and verbally. She was always told how bad she was and how she would never amount to anything because she was so stupid. It didn't matter how hard she tried, she would never measure up to what her parents expected of her. She was very afraid of people, because she expected to be hurt. She always wanted to be hugged, but her fear kept her from getting those hugs she so much desired. She just wanted someone to take care of her, to let her sit on their lap and be rocked, but she could not find that in her family.

The picture I have of Cindy is a small girl in a large dark room, curled up in a ball in a far corner. I look at her and see fear all over her little sweet face. She doesn't say anything, just rocks back and forth. It's as if she wants to talk, but fear overwhelms her and keeps her silent

Cindy was full of questions. She would really make herself known in therapy when Mrs. Smith would mention the name of Jesus. She had never heard of Him before and wanted to learn all she could.

"Does Jesus love me?" she would ask time and time again. "He knows how bad I am, and He still loves me?" This was almost more then her little mind could handle. Sometimes we would spend most of the session talking about Jesus' loving Cindy.

She had never had anyone love her unless they wanted something from her. Then she never knew if she would merit their love or not. Jesus' loving her because He just chose to was a foreign concept. Even though Mrs. Smith told her numerous times about Jesus' love did not mean it was easy to fathom. It was very hard, but finally she did believe this great idea.

While I was in the hospital the first time, an interesting event took place concerning Sally and Cindy. I had a room with the window looking onto another part of the building. I sat there and began to think of the words of my counselor: "How can Sally accept the little girl?" I had no answer.

As I sat on my bed looking out of the window, I began to think of Sally and the little girl. I found it all very amazing. I could see a tree with broken branches that was not very pretty, but back in the far dark corner was someone-the little girl. She was tired, frightened, and in great need of a friend. She had no hopes of any friends because she was labeled BAD. On the other side of this building were picnic tables. It was a very pleasant setting. There stood a little girl, Sally.

For days I would see them, just as if they were really there. They really were to me. My thought was, "How can I help them to be friends? If they don't become friends they will never join."

For a number of days, Sally refused to even look in the direction of the little girl. If caught glancing that way, she would just go closer to the wall so she wouldn't have to see all the hurt that the little girl carried. The little girl wanted Sally to be her friend, but she was afraid Sally wouldn't want to be a part of a bad girl. The little girl watched Sally play. Her heart longed to join her, but Sally never looked her way.

When I was talking to Sally one day, I told her she needed to give the little girl a chance. She could help her be happy and even help her carry her pain, which was too much for just one person. Sally slowly walked back to the picnic benches where she liked to play.

One rainy day the girls wanted to play in the rain. It was fine with me. They both were playing; then Sally began to play with the little girl. They laughed and had a good time. Sally had forgotten the little girl's hurt, and for the first time, so did the little girl. It wasn't long before Sally told the little girl that she would help her with the hurt she was carrying. After that they played together as best of friends. Sally felt some of the hurt, and the little girl was finally able to feel some of the happiness that should have been hers all along.

When I had to change rooms, I told them to come with me, since we were all one person and I would help them the best I could. [*Even now they are not left behind. Maybe this was the beginning of my becoming whole; I wasn't really sure.*] Thank the Lord for showing me a little of how I could start to help myself.

What happened with Sally and the little girl did not give Cindy total peace. I was still having problems accepting Cindy and all that she had shared about Dad. She told of a mean, no good, rotten person. I always remembered him as a quiet and okay dad. He would never win Father of the Year award, but he was okay. I had written letters to Cindy, and she wrote back to me. Here's one I've chosen to share with you:

Dear Kiddo,

I have come time and again, trying to tell you how I feel toward you. Many things pop into my mind letting me know that there is a lot about you I'm still not sure that I like. I am trying to love you as I should. For a very long time I was given negative information. I accepted it with no questions asked. It became very easy not to like you.

As I think of you, I recall how I even hated the day you were born. Time and again the story was told how Mom thought she was only to have one, and then there were two. Of course, you were number two. It did not seem to make Mom and Dad happy, but you had no control over that situation. Who did I become angry with? You're right, it was you. I am so sorry. I knew how much you hurt each time this story was told. I added to your pain by also blaming you. Your little mind was just puzzled at what you did wrong. Precious, you did nothing wrong.

Dad began to abuse you, and I put all the blame on you and didn't want anything to do with you. You were hardly given a chance. Certainly Dad could do no wrong, so it had to be you. I am so sorry I added to your pain. Being held and tickled was something you had always enjoyed, but how quickly all of that changed. I know how each touch and hug became a nightmare. The inability to please Dad drove you to try harder, although you felt it was not right. But he did not ask if you minded. He just demanded and expressed his dis-satisfaction with slaps and punishments. The pain was so great it seemed as if your heart would break. Many nights were spent quietly crying yourself to sleep. I know it was a lonely time. Please, let me help that loneliness disappear. I care how you hurt, and I see those tears. You can cry on my shoulder if you like.

With all the negative attitudes I had toward you, I began to feel you were not worth my efforts or anyone else's. I worked at hiding who you really were, but I am beginning to see how valuable you really are. I know I have a lot of work to do to really except you properly, but I am willing to do that work.

Another thing that needs to be talked about is God's love for you. God has always loved you. It has been really hard for me to admit it, but it is a fact. I have tried very hard, in my own power, to protect you and do the best I can for you, but I realize my best is not always good enough. I have not known just how to give you to God. Maybe deep inside I'm afraid He will hurt you or you will not measure up. I wanted to protect you from any possible rejection. I also feel I have this problem with other people as well. The feeling of rejection or being rejected is so strong that I stand at a distance and hope no one cares to get close. Those walls are beginning to fall, but I have a long way to go.

Kid, I just want what is best for you. I'm really sorry you have suffered all this pain, but I want to help you work through it because you are very special to me. As I have told many children in Sunday School, "God loves you and He made you special." This goes for you too, kid. I am not sure what you need but please help me be sensitive to meeting those needs and helping you get everything settled. I love you very much.

Glenda

Dear Lady,

You are important to me. My intent has never been to hurt you. I know all of this has thrown you for a loop. Many times before I have tried to let you know what had happened, but it just never worked out. I know you do not really know what to think of me. That's okay, because much has been said about me even to the point that I did not like myself. I believe you know I tell the truth even when it causes me to get into trouble.

I know you had a picture of Dad quite different than the one I have been letting you see. I am sorry I had to share such a terrifying experience with you. I only do this because I know you seek to be the best person you can. All of this brewing underneath hinders your progress. It is necessary for both of us to face facts and work through all the pain and sorrow this has brought.

I understand why you do not want me to cry, but it is very selfish because you have a husband who will let you cry whenever you need to. He loves you. PLEASE LOVE ME enough to let me cry and share my feelings. I know that the crying seems to magnify the hurt, but please help me. You're the one now who stands between me and healing. I know how you feel and what makes you react as you do. It was also wrong for people to hurt me. I was robbed of the freedom to feel. All the feelings I had were kept under control, as if they did not exist. If you were to get hurt now, I would think it was fine for you to cry and be mad and even scream. I am only asking to be allowed to express the hurt, anger and whatever else that lies inside. I know you realize the hurt and how deep it goes. That is part of your hesitation. Don't worry, because it will be okay.

I know you should be encouraging me because I am just a kid, but I can also see your hurt. We are in this together; we two make up one. Although Dad did this years ago, the pain is as real as if it were yesterday, or even this morning. This is in the past and needs to be put there, so we can be one whole and get on with life.

Mrs. Smith is a good friend to you. She also says that I am okay--not perfect, but okay. Please let me talk to her or let her hug me. You see, I'm not asking for a whole lot, but my whole being is crying out for help. I know you have a good heart. Please keep this in mind as you think about what I have said. If this was any other little girl, how mad would you be? Who would you be mad at? Would you help them to receive the help they need? PLEASE HELP ME!!!!!!!!!!!!!!!

Little Girl

Cindy would make any normal loving and caring mom and dad proud. She is a true survivor.

PAT was very different. She started out as a little girl, then realizing that being a girl was not good, she did all she could to be considered a boy. Climbing trees and trying to out-do any of the boys was what she was always up to. He also tried to help hurry death along the way. For instance, Pat would climb out on very small branches, trusting they would break and drop him to his death. Boys got special treatment, and Pat figured if he became one of them, he would be special also. I thought I would finally be accepted, but I only fooled myself. I also received a letter from Pat which read like this:

Dear Glenda,

I think your husband and boys are really neat. I talked to the therapist today, and she said it would be okay if I wrote to you. I'm not really sure what to say, but when I talked to the therapist, she said Mom and Dad gave me some wrong rules. I don't know why they would do such a thing, but they did. I am a very serious person, but I am told I don't need to be. I know you let your boys have fun. You even tickle them so they can laugh. I'd like to be able to do that, because I'm tired of being serious all the time. I was wondering, if it weren't too much trouble, if you would allow me to be a part of your family and rules? It would be good to laugh and play without being told NO. I love Mom and Dad but I am tired of the way I get treated. I know it will be hard for me to just forget the rules of my parents, but that is why I need your good rules to put in their place. I think you are a swell person, but if you cannot help me I will understand, and I'll still think you are swell. Please let me know.

Pat

Pat was wanting very much to be accepted just as he was, and I did accept him into my family. It became very much okay for him to just take it easy. I believe God has helped me to make rules in my family that are not so confusing to my children. They know what they should and shouldn't do. Pat just wanted a chance to be a kid, and now he has had that chance.

JACK is a guy I really don't know much about, except that it was his job to help protect and take care of everyone. He was strong and caring in his own way.

RED, the last helper, was more of a free-will, happy-go-lucky person. She wanted my hair to be red, and she liked fellows. She was very relaxed around men and enjoyed them very much. Her aim was to please fellows. She was sexy and very flirty. Whatever a man wanted, she was ready and willing to give, even if she knew it was wrong. She felt like she was a slut or whore, and she wanted to perform in that manner. It was a job keeping her in check, because I wanted to keep myself for Mr. Right.

While in the hospital the helpers decided to write my dad a letter:

Fred,

This is JACK. I know you don't know me, but I certainly know you. I am only one of the others that live inside of Glenda. You left the job of taking care of her to me. You call yourself a man. Well, I disagree. You are not worthy to even be called a man--more like a horrible beast. I'm mad at you because I had to come and fulfill the job you should have been doing. Glenda is all right, and you don't deserve her as your child.

My name is AMBER. I'm as mad as hell at you for what you did. You had me so brainwashed that I believed you were a good man, but now I see you for who you are --a mean, brutal individual. I hold a lot of hurt inside, not just for me, but for Cindy, the one you tortured. You didn't care how little she was, only what was pleasing to you. It was unfair and unjust. All you did to me was ignore me or make fun of me, even helping the others to feel it was okay to do this to me. Just as your very hand had patted my bottom, when I passed by it, I wanted to scream. The looks you gave me said a lot. You did not have to speak any words. I could read the meanness in your face and your eyes. I knew it was all no good, but I still stood up for you because I believed I was the bad one. That's not true. You are a raving maniac.

My name is PAT, the one that longed for death to come quickly. You set a pattern for the boys and they followed. When my brother started touching me, I felt it must have been all right. But it made me mad for him to touch any part of me. The love you showed for the boys made me try hard to be just like them. Climbing trees was something I enjoyed very much. When you sawed down the limb, I was very angry and found another way I could make it up the tree. I felt I had showed you. I climbed the tree when the boys couldn't. Also, the pony that I could and did take care of, you gave away. Because I didn't count. The boys didn't want the pony any more, so off he went. I always hated the fact that I was a nobody.

My name is CINDY. You should know me the best of all. I am the one you sexually abused for so long. You had me fooled into thinking you loved me, but that was not real love. I loved you very much until you kept hurting me. It became a cycle. You hurt me. I felt hate for you. What kind of crazy man are you, to hurt me so badly? I looked up to you, only to find out I was admiring a monster, like on some horrible television program.

I'm RED, the one you always said I would be, the one who wanted to make your saying come true. I worked hard to convince Glenda she was a slut and that she was worthless, but I could not get her to listen. She believed the worthless part, but she tried hard not to believe the other. There were a few times I almost won, but I never did. I was never a slut or a whore as you seemed to think. I hated every time you called me those names because it was not true.

SALLY is my name. I'm glad I escaped your wrath. I ran away when I saw how mean you were to Cindy. I wanted to be your little princess, but there was no way.

I'm sure you're wondering what this is all about. These are my helpers. They helped me live through the torture you put me through. I hated the fact that because of one person, I had to have many to fill the place instead of one. It angers me to even think of you now. I even felt good about tearing up your picture.

You caused my life to be like hell on earth. Many times, even as an adult, this has crept into my life and caused trouble. I didn't even know what was causing all the problems. Now that I know, I'm working at correcting them. You are not going to win; I am, because there are people who love me who are willing to help me work through all the pain and anguish of the terrible past. God is also here very near to help in every way. I'm a survivor!!!

Glenda and Company

Now that you know me in my entirety, we will move on to more therapy and how things worked out.

Chapter 4

WORK, WORK, WORK

Janet was surprised when I took being MPD in stride. I figured it was a fact that could not be argued with--at least until I figured out what it really meant. I had no idea about all the work that would be involved. I was willing to work but never knew it would be so hard.

Work, work, work--that was all that was on my mind. Even when I went to bed I tried to determine how I could do more and better tomorrow. Sleep wasn't easy to come by since I had to work even as I tried to sleep. Janet or Mrs. Smith hadn't told me to work all the time. That was my own idea. I wanted to get done. The harder I worked, the sooner I would be done; so I pushed on.

Janet wanted to meet the alters. I wasn't really sure about this, but she assured me it was necessary. Even though I was disassociating, I still did not want to own up to the fact that I had little control over the situation. Before long it became very evident that the alters were coming--with or without my permission. I felt frightened because I didn't know what would happen. I trusted Janet, but I wasn't sure what my alters would tell. I wasn't sure I wanted to know any more. I felt I knew enough.

I began to realize some of the time when they would be coming. I would blink my eyes really hard, as if to get rid of myself. Then, there someone would be. I didn't always know what went on, but sometimes I did remember little pieces. I remember trying not to blink so that I could stay around, but it didn't work. The harder I tried to stay, the more I left.

It seems that Janet talked most to Cindy. As reference was made earlier, Janet was the one who helped her have a name from the story I had written. Cindy was never quite sure whom to trust, so she was always fearful. The fear would show on my face and even in the way I held my whole body.

One day while Cindy was talking to Janet, there was a very loud noise outside the office door. It put fear in Cindy like the fear she had experienced as a child. She did the only thing she knew to do. Hurrying from the chair to the floor, she curled up in a corner and shook.

It took quite awhile before Janet could convince me it was safe. I slowly came from the corner, but Cindy didn't stay around. She wasn't convinced that this place was safe. Even when I came back later to Janet's office, I felt some of that fear. Janet was very sorry it happened, but there was nothing she could have done. I understand now, but at the time I was unsure if I'd be able to trust that place again.

There was even a playroom in the building. We spent some time in there. It was a very interesting place with dolls, a sand box, kitchen set, and table. We could color. There were little people, a ball, and other things one would find in a toy room. I enjoyed going in there. It was okay to be a kid there, and that is what I would become. Janet would even talk to the alters there, and they felt freer to talk in such a relaxing place.

One time we sat and colored, making a picture. Mine was just scribble marks on the paper, but I was proud. Janet drew me a picture of a tree with a little pond by it and a duck in the pond. I thought that was great. To me, it was a beautiful picture. I felt honored that she would give it to me. I brought it home and put it on my refrigerator. Different times during the day I found myself just looking at it. I wanted to be able to draw like that.

I remember going into the playroom one day and playing in the sand box. There were little men. Some were soldiers who had been wounded. Others looked like farmers. There were also horses and trees. I had the men fighting for awhile, falling from their horses. I would lay some of them under the shade tree as they rested.

When I found one of the men that reminded me of my dad, the play began to change. I buried him and had the horses run over him. I didn't want something that looked like him to be around. I also buried others that were hurt. Digging them up, I would try to take care of them. If I dug up Dad by mistake, I became angry and buried him again. Before I left that day, I had saved everyone but Dad. I did not want him around any more, so I left him under the sand. I guess it was my way of trying to get rid of him.

I had brought a picture of my dad to therapy and one day Janet brought it to the playroom. Not knowing what was going to happen, she gave me the picture and went to a room where she could watch. For awhile I just sat there and looked at it. It almost felt like he was right there. Janet had said if I needed her I just had to let her know, and she would come back in. After I sat in a daze looking at the picture I forgot Janet was even around.
I found a stick, and at first I just hit myself very lightly with it. Anger began to rise within me. I then began to hit the picture. At first it was not very hard, because I was still a little afraid of Dad. You have to realize that to me, as I sat there on the floor, this picture was more than just a picture. It was my dad. I began to feel the anger take over and there was nothing I could do. I hit the picture harder and harder. After awhile the picture

was in pieces. The smaller the pieces, the better I felt. I then began to shed a few tears which was very different for me. There lay these pieces of paper all over the floor where I sat and I just sat there.

Janet came in and said: "What a good job." I felt like I had lost; I'm not sure why, but I didn't feel pleased with myself. A lot of the time I pushed on because of Janet and Mrs. Smith telling me I was doing well. My evaluation was not always very good, but I trusted them and went by what they had to say.

Mrs. Smith met me at Janet's office one time. She talked to Janet while I waited in the playroom. After a few minutes, they came in the playroom as well. This time Amber came. It was a time of fighting--her strength against Janet's. Amber was very angry and didn't care who knew it. Janet had been telling Amber that suicide was no answer. If she killed herself, she also would be killing everyone else and that would be unfair to the others. They didn't want to die. Somewhere along the line Janet had my hand and we were struggling. I probably wanted to hit her and she was defending herself. I'm not really sure. I do remember she was very strong and not willing to let me go. I know Amber had her work cut out for her.

Amber didn't want to leave that day. She wanted to take total control. Mrs. Smith was taking me home afterwards. She told Janet that I had to come back before she could leave, because Amber was too strong for her. Amber wasn't pleased with that information, but she finally did leave so I could go home. At this point, Amber was ready to rule my life and take it all at the same time. She thought I wasn't able to function any longer, and she had a solution as always--death.

Not only were things very hard for me, they had to be difficult for my therapist as well. She would never know who was coming to sessions or how many, so every session was a guessing time for her. I did have an advantage over her--there were more of me than of her. She didn't complain, but stuck with me through the good and the bad. She didn't get upset with the alters, but tried to help them see how things really were, which was a big job. She had her work cut out for her, just as mine was cut out for me.

All of this work didn't make things disappear; it helped me see there was a lot more work to do. At that point I was not thinking very straight, so I wasn't even very aware of the situation around me. Everything was hard, and sessions were like nightmares. I dissociated so much I hardly knew if I was coming or going. I would also have to stay longer just so I could come back before I left the building. I felt the therapists couldn't do anything more for me.

Life again looked very bleak. Amber's idea looked better and better. My thoughts again turned to suicide more and more. I tried not to talk about it because it upset everyone so much. I don't remember telling anyone how I felt, but I had talked to Gloria. She knew from our conversation and called my husband. Out of concern, he called Janet and told her.

I went to session like always, not knowing that anyone knew what was going on in my mind. Janet began to ask how I felt. Of course I said I was fine, as I always did. Then somehow she asked me if I was having any thoughts about hurting myself. I must have told her yes, because she wanted to talk to my husband. When my husband came to pick me up that day, he came into the office. He wasn't surprised when she shared with him. I had hoped he would throw a fit because she wanted me to go to the hospital. Oh no, he agreed with her conclusion. At the time I just gave up inside myself because I was beyond help anyway. That's how I saw things.

This decision wasn't one we took lightly, but it also wasn't one we talked about. Janet told him how to go through the channels to get me into the State Hospital. We had no insurance, so we had no other recourse. I didn't put up a fight. I didn't seem to care; I was like a whipped pup. I promised I would work harder if I could only stay at home, but that wasn't the problem. We met with the judge, who said they would put me on the waiting list for the next possible bed. When a bed came open they were to call us.

Now I just needed to wait. I still went to therapy and waited my time out. My husband stayed home with me most of the time, because he didn't know what I would do. He took all the knives out of the kitchen. It was very frustrating to want to cut an onion and not remember how or not be able to find a knife to do so.

We had told our children that I had to go to the hospital. We had everything worked out for them to be taken care of. Gloria said she would take care of our boys whenever we needed her to. My mind was at peace knowing my children would be taken care of properly.

Before I went into the hospital, I felt like I needed to tell everyone good bye. I guess I was not sure if I would ever come out again. My therapist assured me things would be fine and I would be able to come home as soon as I was able. I did not feel reassured, but I continued to wait.

Chapter 5

OFF I GO

As the days passed, I was very anxious whenever the phone rang. I was always sure the day had come. But the days turned into weeks, and not just one week passed, but three. I was sure they had not forgotten me, because it did not seem to be the thing they would do.

Finally the call came. I was to go the next day. It was a long and fearful night. My restlessness was due to uncertainty about what lay ahead.

In quietness my husband and I traveled to the hospital. Our hearts were heavy because we knew I would be there at least three weeks. Knowing the time would be long, we had already begun to miss each other. As they checked in my luggage I looked at my husband, as if to say, “Please, don't leave me here.” My husband's heart was also breaking. He didn’t want to leave me, but it had to be done. While going to the building where I was to make my home for the next ninety-five days, I was unaware that I would not see my husband for the next seven days. I didn't even get to tell him good-bye.

I tried to be brave, but I could see it wasn’t working. I was ushered into Ward One, where I took a shower and changed into one of the hospital gowns. Afterwards I was taken to a small room where I met with my treatment team. I certainly wanted my husband there, because he had always been there to help me. I was told he had left. I felt totally abandoned. I wanted to run. I felt like it was all hopeless; now it was over. My heart sank to my toes. What was I going to do now?

The meeting went on. The thing I remember the most was the noise, and the fear someone might touch me and hurt me. I examined the faces of those who asked me questions, looking for someone to help. My eyes went from one person to the next, trying to find help as I did my best to answer their many questions. My eyes rested on a red-headed lady (*whom I will call Dr. Red*). There seemed to be something special about her. It appeared that she could read my mind, but at that point it was no big job.

They asked me about being MPD and wanted me to tell them what that meant. I was a little confused because I thought they should know, or else how could they help me? Most of them had something to say, but not Dr. Red. She sat there in silence, but her looks spoke volumes. The interview was hard because the noise seemed to be so great. I could hardly concentrate.

It was over. I was put on Ward One for only a short while, then moved on to Ward Two. I spent one night there and moved on to Ward Four. I began to feel things were going fine and that I'd soon be out of the hospital. My spirits were lifted.

I faithfully went to all the activities I was supposed to attend, but a problem began to surface. I had worked hard at not letting things bother me. The pace became too much. I needed to rest to continue the fooling I was doing. When the doctor made his rounds, I had been laughing with another patient and seemed to be having a good time. He appeared to be pleased.

Before he left I caught him by the door where I could have some privacy, because I really needed to talk to him. They kept our rooms locked in the afternoon so we would go to the activities. They wanted us to stay active. I asked the doctor if he could just let me rest. I was beginning to not function very well. I knew I was losing it again. I didn't want to tell him all of this. He didn't want me to lie down.

His solution was to make an appointment for me with my psychologist, Shirley. He thought it would be good if I explained to her my problem. Nervously, I went for a walk with the other ladies from the ward. Uncertain what was going to happen, I fidgeted around until Shirley came to talk.

When I saw Shirley arrive, I wanted to hide, but there was no place to run. We found our way to an office and began to talk. I didn't want to volunteer any information, but they said I had to talk. She said she could see the hurt in my eyes, and she wanted me to tell her about it. After a great hesitation I began to tell her how I was really feeling. At that point I was becoming very suicidal again. I told her about the iron in our quiet room, and how the cord would be something I could use. I didn't realize what I was saying, except that I was being extremely honest. When we went back to the ward, she had the iron removed and left.

I thought now they would let me sleep. Then things would be fine again. I was in for a big surprise. Shirley soon returned and said she and the doctor wanted to talk to me. Off we went again to an office. They had talked about my situation and decided I needed to return to Ward One on suicide watch. Needless to say, this did not make me happy. Off I went to Ward One anyway.

I'm sure you have guessed that my stay on Ward One this time was not a short one, and you are right. I was fooling no one. Dr. Red came to see me. She said she was going to be my therapist. All I wanted her to do was get me off that ward, so I could prepare to go home. Three weeks had passed and no release was in sight. I finally decided that all my talking would not get me out, so I might as well settle in for the duration.

I was angry at everyone and didn't know whom to trust. I trusted Shirley and look what happened. Now who was I to trust? Dr. Red said I could trust the staff, and that they only did this for my safety. Do you think I believed her? No way. I wasn't afraid of anyone. If they wanted a fight, I would be glad to help them out, but I didn't start things.

One big lady was always looking for a fight. The others were afraid of her. I didn't have enough sense to be. I stood toe to toe with her, and at first she laughed at me. She probably thought that because she was about twice my size I was the funniest thing she had met. We became friends, and I tried to help her stay out of trouble. Whenever she got into an argument with someone, I tried to calm her down and we would walk away laughing.

After a number of days I got moved to Ward Two. Activity began to increase. I had sessions with Shirley and Dr. Red. If I wasn't meeting with one, I was seeing the other. I don't remember why we started having sessions together, but I am told I asked for it. Boy, was that a mistake--a double whammy. These ladies were good. What one didn't think of, the other did. It was some combination. At first, it was hard to open up. They had to convince me it was safe and that they would still accept me. You would think this would have been settled already since I had already seen two therapists, but each new person had to assure me.

I've always had the feeling that I was to be the one helping others--receiving help was very strange. I did help the workers some. At times I was mistaken for an employee, instead of a patient. All of this was fine to a point, but it began to interfere with my progress. It was much easier to concentrate on others than on myself. Dr. Red told me not to help the other patients. The workers were to assist them. I needed to take care of myself. This became a time of hard work.

Things seemed to be going very fast, and I became very frustrated. The staff were trying to help me deal with the anger. I was unable--or unwilling--to let myself deal with this issue. Instead of dealing with it in therapy where I was supposed to, I began to get angry with the ladies on the ward. I was misdirecting my anger, as I had always done. This was because the thing I was really angry about was too hard to face. Finally I was able to deal with the issue. Saying it was hard is putting it very mildly.

After what seemed like a lifetime on Ward Two, I got moved to Ward Four. There were more activities to do on Ward Four, and I told my doctor if I had to keep the pace I had in therapy, I could not attend all the activities. He was very understanding and allowed me to miss some things. In sessions I began to reveal who I really was, and that was frightful. My fear was always that they would give up on me. Although they never gave me any reason to think that, those were still my thoughts.

One of the assignments that I was given was to write down the abuse in detail, as I remembered it. I was sure they could not be serious, Dr. Red was quick to let me know they were very serious. I explained to them that I had already done that, and I didn't care to do it again. Moping back in my room, I thought that being sexually abused should have been enough. Fear was running wild within me. Struggling to find the right words to describe the horror that took place was not easy, even though I had done it one time already.

Returning to session with paper in hand, I handed it to Dr. Red. She handed it back to me and wanted me to read it. I just couldn't. They began to tell me all the reasons why I should, and I continued to tell them I just couldn't. The issue seemed to be one of secrecy--this was my secret. I couldn’t tell it. If I told it out loud, that would be the worst.

I wanted to do what they said, but I just couldn't bring myself to read or just tell what I had written. I had built up my confidence in them, but I felt they had stepped over the line. After a very long while I began to speak the words. As I spoke, it was as if my heart was being torn out. In detail I recalled the terrible soul-ripping events that had caused me so much pain and sorrow. I thought that would be the hardest thing I would ever have to do. The surprise was on me, because many hard things followed.

The helpers began to make themselves known. Again, there are a lot of those times I do not remember. I recall them being long hard times of work. Each helper had his or her own story to tell. Some more than others, but they took their turns expressing their feelings. I found it hard to just let go and let them do their thing, partly because I was not sure what they would do and partly because I thought they would cry and look foolish. Whatever my reason, it made things very difficult and fearful.

One session when Cindy was sharing, Dr. Red discovered that I liked rabbits. A few days later, she gave me a stuffed bunny. It had been played with and it was worn, but to me it was beautiful. Dr. Red said I could keep it. I found that to be very amazing, that she would give me such a precious item. She also said it was full of love; that children had played with it and it had had plenty of love. I proudly took it back to my room, and it became my best friend. When I was troubled at night, I would sleep with it and feel the love it possessed. She was right. It was full of love. It didn'tt solve my problems, but it helped me to remember I was loved.

We talked for many hours on end, but it seemed to be getting us no place. Action was needed and finally taken. I had brought in pictures of my parents. The staff made copies for some activities. I was never sure what would happen in sessions. It became one surprise after another.

One day we went outside. With them they carried a trash bag full of something. When we arrived at a bench, they began to pull out balloons with my dad's picture on the front of them. Taping them to the bench, they gave me darts to throw at the balloons. I thought this was silly and put very little effort into the throws. Dr. Red and Shirley kept telling me to throw them harder. Before long I was doing just that. I didn't think about who might see or how silly I might look. I even began enjoying the pop the balloons made.

The pictures stayed intact. As I picked up the pieces of balloons and put them in the trash bag, I also picked up the pictures. Dr. Red said, "Why don't you tear them up before you throw them away?" I began to tear them into little pieces and throw them into the trash. It felt great to destroy the picture of the man who caused me such heartache. As I went back to my room that day, I felt relief for a job well done.

Another exercise we did outside was screaming. This was to help me learn how to get rid of tension, I think. Shirley was leading this session. She would scream, then we--Dr. Red and I--were supposed to repeat it. Dr. Red did a very good job, but I just could not bring myself to scream. After the exercise went on for awhile, and with their insistence, I finally brought myself to scream. It wasn't as loud as they wanted, but it was satisfactory. I went back to my room feeling like I had let them down. I promised myself I would try harder next time.

An exercise I did to help me feel anger was to write a letter to Dad from the helpers (*recorded in a previous chapter*). After I had this letter written, Dr. Red and I went to a little theater on the grounds. We were on the stage. Then she left me there and took her seat in the audience. I was to read what I had written. I read the letter one time, then stopped. I hadn't read it with much force.

She put something in the chair next to her and said to pretend that it was my Dad, and that I wanted him to be sure to hear what I had to say. I had only read a little. She stopped me, saying she didn't want to sit so close to him, and moved the thing over a couple of chairs.

"Now," she said, "read the letter with all the feeling you have, telling him how you feel." I was able to read my letter with more force, and feel angry that because of his actions I became MPD. It was a sobering experience.

There were times that were less stressful, such as taking walks. We would go out by the water and throw sticks in, or see how far we could throw stones. This was an exercise I could get into. The feeling of running was pretty much gone. However, I found it easier to talk outside. There is something freeing about the outdoors for me. One time while Dr. Red and I were walking, I began to tell her about Sally. As I talked I felt very proud of such a young girl. We also talked about my family. It was like all inhibitions had flown away. Inside, my words just bounced around on the walls and hit you in the face again.

About this time I was moved to Ward Five. This was the ward on which everyone wanted to be. This meant you were on your way out or were ready to move on. I was definitely ready to move right on home. They were still not ready to release me I was beginning to think they just must like my company.I liked their company, also, but if that was all it was, I could come back and visit them. This wasn't the case; I had more work to do. I continued my work, but things seemed to be turning from good to bad. Sometimes it became confusing.

Anger was always something with which I constantly had to work. I was always finding ways to misdirect the anger I had. One day while my husband and I were visiting in the ward lobby because of the rain outside, I had a run-in with one of the other ladies. My husband and I were laughing and having as good a time as possible. One of the ladies came around the corner and accused us of spying on her. There was no reasoning with her. She continued to go on and on. I became angry. My husband and I did not get to see each other often, so I wanted her to leave us alone.

Off of my chair I came, ready to let her have it. A worker stopped me. She treated me as if I was in the wrong. I wanted her to know I wasn't putting up with this any more. My husband and I finished our visit in another room. I was furious and crying all at the same time. My husband was so surprised. He said he had never seen me so mad before.

When he left I was still a basket case. I went to my room and wanted to scream. Instead I laid down and covered up from my head to my toes. It was supposed to be a sign for no one to bother me, but some people don't take a hint. I had permission to call Dr. Red anytime I wanted, and I was feeling I really needed to talk now. It was Saturday and I didn't want to disturb her at home, so I tried to hide.

After the incident, the weekend went slower then normal. Monday finally came, and I asked to see her. She sat down in the chair, and I began to tell her what happened Saturday and how angry I had become. She was smiling and laughing and hollering, "Yea!" She was happy that I had become angry and cried. I told her it was not funny, but she was so excited that before long I forgot I was mad and laughed with her. She said this is what they had been trying to get me to do, but not at the patients. She wasn't mad at me for getting upset with a patient. She even said she would bale me out if I got into trouble. It was understood that I was not to hit anyone, or I would be in big trouble from which she could not get me out. I took her at her word and continued in therapy.

Another written assignment came my way. I was to write all the bad or negative things my mom or dad said to me. I figured that would be easy. Within two hours I had forty things listed. Just writing them down made me feel frustrated with my parents, because it sounded like they said nothing good. I thought for a while and couldn't come up with anything good. Some of the things I did come up with were: You're stupid, you're ugly, you're fat, you'll never amount to anything, you're lazy, you're a slut, etc. These are not things to say to someone if you are trying to help them build a good self image. I gave my list to Dr. Red and waited to see what she had planned.

After a couple of weeks I was to find out her plan. This is something that I probably will never forget. When I walked into her office, Shirley was also sitting there, and things appeared pretty much like normal. The shades were pulled, the lights were off, and a candle was lit. I was sure I was ready for anything. She had me lie down on the couch and get relaxed. She talked to me in a soft, gentle tone. I found myself relaxing. I thought this was great, because I was somewhat tired. I was in a state of total relaxation.

To my surprise, she began to play a tape recorder on which were some of the sayings I had given to her. I began to hear the words of my father. Cindy was there. Although the man's voice on the tape was no one I knew, it sounded to me like my dad. It scared me so badly that I thought I would have a heart attack. My first and strongest reaction was to run.

Shirley told me he was tied up in a chair and could not hurt me. When she turned the tape recorder off, she said they had gagged him. She wanted me to tell him how mad I was, but there was no yelling in me. I was brave when the tape recorder was off, but on it came again. I asked her to gag him again. She said she couldn't. I told her we should run away and hide because he would hurt us, but she would not go. She said the only way he would shut up was for me to yell and tell him how angry I was at him. The tape played on as she did her best to convince me that everything was safe and he couldn't touch me.

I was finally able to start yelling very softly. It was more like requesting. The tape kept right on going, and I was reminded that he was hard of hearing. I was concerned for everyone's safety, and I gradually began to yell louder and louder, expressing my displeasure with him. I told him how angry I was, and how he had no right to treat me like he did or call me the names he had called me. It must have been loud enough because the tape went off.

I was relieved and very tired. He was gone out of the room and I could rest. He would never be able to bother me again. I truly could rest. I felt for the first time that Cindy was able to get free. The experience was so real I was sure they had taken him out of the room before I opened my eyes. When I opened my eyes, there were only my two dear friends.

Things began to look up. There was talk of my discharge. Needless to say, I was really excited. We talked about a finality. Options were being given, and my mind tried to quickly evaluate each one. As soon as I heard the one about burning an effigy of my Dad, that sounded great to me. It was settled. Plans began to be made for this event.

One day I came into the office and there lay a pair of bib overalls. Dad wore these all the time. I wanted to run out--you would have thought the pants were going to attack me. Things were not coming together as I had hoped. It was becoming a problem. I told my doctor to tell Dr. Red to forget it. We would do something else. His response was, "Are you not worth the effort?" That is not what I had meant, but that is what I had said, in my own way.

Every time I came into the office after they had those pants I found it hard to concentrate. My mind was more on the pants. Previously, the feeling of wanting to run had often been within me. Now it was no different.

Shirley would say, "Do you want to go back to the old world?" I was constantly reminded of what I was trying to free myself. One time when I came into the office, I noticed when the door was closed, the bibs were hanging there along with a picture of my folks. They told me if I ran, it would be going back to the old world. I certainly didn't want that. It was hard to go on with this treatment. I didn't want to lose my parents, and I felt like that was what was happening.

My doctor came in one day close to time for me to get out and wanted to know how things were going. Of course I said, "fine." I didn't want to say anything that would keep me any longer. I asked him what would happen if I was not ready to go in two weeks as planned. He told me I would have to stay for another year. My heart skipped a beat. Then we both kind of laughed. After he left, a friend of mine wanted to know if he was serious. I assured her he was not, but deep inside I was not sure. We had often teased each other. I was hoping this was just another one of those times. I did try to work harder the next two weeks. I didn't want to take any chances.

I was leaving the hospital as scheduled, but we couldn't do the finality because of the rain. I was already scheduled for a two week evaluation, so plans were made for this to take place then. While I was home for those two weeks, I thought about the finality all the time. I even began to dream about it. Two weeks couldn't pass fast enough. The day finally came. As I got ready to return for my finality, my husband said, "Think of this as your Independence Day."

My husband dropped me off at the hospital. I was to call him when it was over. I was nervous as I waited for Shirley and Dr. Red. When Shirley arrived, she escorted me to Dr. Red's office. To my shock there was a figure representing Dad. It was about the same height as he was, dressed like he had dressed many times with a plaid shirt, bib overalls, and white socks. It had a balloon for a head with his picture on it and cigarettes in his upper pocket. They had done a very good job. I felt ready to run, but out the corner of my eye I saw Dr. Red standing in the doorway. If I ran I would have to knock her down. I did not think that was a good idea. Standing there breathless, I just stared at this figure. It was time to go to our site.

Shirley and I rode in the van, and Dr. Red came with the fireman in a truck. As we rode, I was telling my friend about seeing the movie Star Trek Generations. In the movie, Data (the android) had a feeling chip inserted because he always wanted to be able to feel. Then he could feel. What a shock he was in for--not only did he have the good feelings, he also had the bad. He was not sure he wanted the chip anymore because of the bad feelings.

At this point, I could really relate to that, because I was having all kinds of feelings I had never had before. These feelings were new to me as well as to Data, and I was told to "feel the feelings". “Feel the feelings” was probably their favorite phrase, because I heard it probably a hundred times or more. Since I was not used to feeling, it was scary, but I kept trying.

Shirley and I had a good chuckle as we arrived. We walked around and talked as we waited for Dr. Red to arrive. I was wondering if I was doing the right thing. She was sure I was. She told me to think of this just as my husband had, as my independence day. She had also brought a tape with the song, "Independence Day."

When Dr. Red arrived, she got the figure out of the truck and laid it on the ground. I sat it up; then we were ready. They said I could do whatever I wanted. Of course, you can probably guess--I said I wanted to run. They wanted me to put the kerosene on the effigy and light it, but I found myself very frightened. I just couldn’t do it.

They began to play the tape with all of those negative sayings on it. I really wanted to run then, but they assured me this was necessary for my healing. I argued. Shirley said I sounded just like my dad. That made me angry, because I never wanted to sound like him or act like him. I took the kerosene, poured it on, and lit the figure. They turned off the tape of the sayings and put on the tape of the song "Independence Day". It burned well, and I sat down right in front of it. As it burned, I took deep breaths while each of the helpers said their good-byes. When the burning stopped, I beat the frame until I was sure all was over. What a release!

The three of us made our way back to the building. As I walked, my steps seemed to be lighter. The farther I walked the freer I felt. Getting back to the building, I called my husband and he came after me. As I waited for him, I said my good-byes to some friends. Then I needed to get some things I had left in Dr. Red's office.

When I got to her office, she was in a meeting, but she graciously asked me in. The people in her office were looking at a book I had brought. I gave my good friends a hug and began to leave the room. Stopping in the doorway, I wanted to know if I was discharged now. Their answer was yes. I was so excited. I very loudly said "Yes!" with my fist coming down as I spoke.

Now all that was left was waiting on my husband. He soon came, and off I went to be home with my family again.

Chapter 6

I'VE ARRIVED, I'VE ARRIVED

I've arrived, I've arrived, I've arrived. I will go to therapy and attend a support group, but I have arrived. No more problems, no more trouble. I am better. I have been healed. No more hard work, and nothing can touch me now. Smooth sailing from here on out. These were my thoughts as I finished my work at the hospital. I was a new person.

I started going back to Janet for therapy once a week. Soon it was moved to every other week. It was hard going back to her after being out of contact for three and a half months. I thought everything would run smoothly, and in a few short weeks I'd finally be finished.

Things did not go as I expected. We played catch-up on my hospital experience. I eagerly told of the things I could remember, and especially the things that I felt had helped. It was not long before I began to have trouble. I would call the hospital and talk to Dr. Red, but I was keeping myself torn between her and Janet. I did not see what I was doing at first, then Dr. Red and Shirley helped me to understand that this was not healthy. I then began to try hard to focus on the therapy

I was receiving from Janet. Things began to settle down, my trouble wasn't over.

I began to have a variety of feelings. Since I was not used to expressing them, it was very uncomfortable. Janet encouraged me to express these feelings and not to be afraid of them. I thought that I was still afraid of my feelings, but I really was not.

I became angry at what my dad had done, but was unsure how to deal with this. Janet gave me an assignment--I was to write down two ways I could express my anger, then read it twice a day. I laughed, but I really saw nothing funny. I just thought this couldn't be real, but it was. I went home stewing and thinking it was ridiculous, but I sat down and wrote. It was as hard as I thought. I read it every day twice until I felt I could handle no more. I called Janet and told her I just couldn't do it anymore. I thought she would give me a break, but she just said to keep on doing the assignment.

I hung up the phone angry with her, but I kept on reading. It really did help. When I went back to see her I told her it had worked. We had a good laugh together, because I had been proven wrong. I guess that should have taught me not to question her methods, but I learn the hard way.

During this time I started going to a support group as well. As I prepared for the first meeting, I remember thinking this was supposed to help me. I was a nervous wreck. I arrived and found just a few ladies there. Still, that did not settle my fear. I tried to find a seat far away from everyone, but it was impossible. It was a very small room with chairs all around. Finally, I did take a seat. I sat as stiff as a board, almost afraid to breathe. Others began to share, and they all appeared relaxed. I'm sure they could tell I was in no way relaxed. The lady sitting on my right leaned down to scratch her leg, and I just about jumped out of my shoes. I was afraid she was going to grab me or something. She had no intention of even touching me. She was really a sweet lady. At the time I was not sure of anything or anyone.

I talked to the group leader afterwards and asked her if it would be proper for me to share what had happened to me. I wanted reassurance that no one would laugh at me and that I would still be accepted. At the second meeting, the group leader asked me if I had something I wanted to share. With fear and trembling, I briefly told my sad story and waited for the group members to tell me how awful I was. To my surprise, there was no such response. Instead they were loving and caring. The fear of rejection was quickly fleeing as they made me feel important. I began to feel that I belonged someplace. I was accepted just as I was. There were not too many people that I felt accepted me that way. It was a refreshing feeling.

As I continued in therapy, I realized I was afraid of looking or feeling feminine. I expressed this to Janet, and of course she gave me another assignment. For fifteen minutes a day, I was to put on this dress that made me feel feminine. I had gotten it just before I went to the hospital. This was to be done every day until I saw her again, in two weeks. I could not believe my ears. She also said I could wear it to the next session if I wanted. I laughed, thinking this surely was a joke, but I asked her if she was serious. She said she was as serious as a heart attack. I thought you couldn't get any more serious than that. As she was writing my appointment card for the next time, she said, "Here I am doing good therapy, and you don't even appreciate it." As I drove home, I found her comment to be amusing, because I knew she was a good therapist. She only had me do what she felt was best for my healing.

During the next two weeks, I played dress-up during the day while I was home by myself. I even began to like having a dress on. I didn't look half bad. When I went back for my next appointment, I walked in with my special dress on. I think Janet was a little surprised, but pleased. I felt proud of myself. I really liked the way I looked, for the first time. I am no beauty queen, but that day I felt like I was a princess. I don't think anyone could have told me different. I still had a little problem with the guys who looked at me, but I would learn to handle that also.

Group was going along well, and I found it becoming easier to share. At first some of my sharing was done through writing. It was easier to express myself that way. My stories were received very well. The ladies even said the stories helped them. I began to feel more confident of myself. I found it to be a great relief to find someone else who understood what it was like to be sexually abused. Sometimes it is easy to see our own problems as being gigantic. When you hear someone else speak who has had it just as bad or worse than you, it puts a whole new dimension on your own problems.

Things began to click as I began to read through the journal that I had kept through my therapy. I began to see how much progress I had made. It was different to see it for myself. Others had told me I was making progress, but until I saw it myself it was unbelievable.

I still had things to work through. Yes, I was making real progress. I was beginning to get used to this wholeness, although there were still some problems. The more I let the feelings happen, the more comfortable

I felt with the feelings. I was becoming comfortable with life. The real world was not all that bad. There is real joy as well as sorrow, real happiness as well as pain. Life is not all one big mess. It has its showers of peace and contentment. God has designed things very well. I'm sure He was glad I approved.

In Janet's and my therapy sessions, things were really different. One session she made me upset, and at the end of the session she began to laugh. Not seeing anything funny, I inquired what was funny. She began to explain to me how during this session I had showed a variety of emotions--anger, teary eyes, and a couple of other feelings. She was pleased I was showing my feelings. She said Dr. Red would be proud of me. I felt all puffed up and proud of myself.

Other times in session she would smile and say "You would have never acted like that a year ago." She was making reference to the fact that I was calmer and more collected when things went wrong at home. She kept saying I was doing well, and I was beginning to believe her. She is a great therapist. She has patience and a good sense of humor, which I think is important.

Something mentioned earlier was the issue of forgiveness. I want to add a few last words about the subject. Forgiveness is important to me, not for my dad's sake, but for mine. Holding on to resentment only eats at me and makes my life miserable. Complete healing came only when my attitude of forgiveness took place. Have I forgiven my dad? Yes, I do believe I have. Even though the terror of my life will always be in my memory. Putting that terror in the past and having it as a memory that does not haunt my every moment helps me to live in the here and now. This is where I want to be.

Changing one's ways of thinking about oneself is important. Most people I have come across who have been abused have a poor self image. The degradation of the abuse helps feed this kind of image. There is hope. You can by the help of God, change the image you have of yourself. It involves self-talk in a positive way. We are used to telling ourselves how bad we are, but we need to start telling ourselves how good we are. If there are things about yourself you don't like and you can change them, then change them. If you cannot change them, learn to accept them and go on.

As you read this you might think, "That's easy for her to say." Believe me, I know how hard it can be. I am working on these things myself. I have a job just letting myself know I'm okay. God made me and He doesn't make junk. Those in my background who worked at destroying me will not win the battle, by God's help.

"In order to become healthy, to become all that you were created to be, the only answer is that you must digest certain key truths. You need to hear the facts. You need to soak for awhile in the healing balm of God's word."[4] God is there for us; He cares and loves us. It is important that we understand His love and His word, because it will help speed our recovery.

Something Beautiful

Something beautiful
Something good
All of my confusion
He understood
All I had to offer Him
Was brokeness and strife,
But He made something
Beautiful of my life.

Psalm 17:8 "Keep me as the apple of Your eye; Hide me under the shadow of Your wings." (*New King James Version*)

4Bill Ritchie, A Dad Who Loves You (Sisters: Multnomah Press Books, 1992), p. 17.

Chapter 7

STRAIGHT FROM THE HORSE'S MOUTH

This chapter will be informative, because it views the abused from the eyes of a close bystander. My husband has graciously consented to give us insight into the life he saw and led during these past three years. We will address this in a question and answer format.

Q. *What were your feelings when you first found out I was going to counseling? Were you aware there was such a serious problem?*

A. I remember that day very well. I got a message from the office saying I had an important phone call and I needed to call this number. When I called that number, Mrs. Smith told me who she was and said you had been seeing her for three or four months. I thought, "WOW." You were suicidal. It was either call me or the police. I'm glad she chose me. It's funny because I told my boss I needed to go home right away, there was a problem. Just because of my tone of voice and my body language, he said, "Go, and we'll be praying for you." I left and came home. First, I was fearful you would do something to yourself before I could get home. I remember driving very fast and trying to remind myself to be careful. When I got home you were in the bedroom with the curtains pulled and the light off, just sitting in the dark. You were very sullen. I just wanted to help comfort you and support you any way I could.

There was no problem with you going to a counselor. It was okay with me. I didn't think any less of you or think you were a weak person. I think it takes a lot of courage, an inner strength, to go to a counselor. God gives you that strength. It's like when you are sick, you go to the doctor. When you are emotionally sick, you get the help needed. I could have ranted and raved, but what good would that have done? As a Christian I think that would almost be a sin. Certainly the Lord had to be working on me not to react in a negative way. It really drives home, becoming one flesh.

Q. *What were your inner thoughts when you found out about the sexual abuse?*

A. Somehow I knew, and if you remember correctly, I asked if it was your Dad (*I don't remember*). It didn't surprise me; it didn't shock me. I just hurt for you because I saw how you were reacting and how you were behaving. You were just so fearful that I would reject you. You tried and tried and tested me. We would be rich people if we got money for all the times you tried and tested me. You would remember something else and would tell me, as if that would stop me from loving you.

You are stuck with me. Remember our wedding vows--"for richer and poorer, in sickness and in health, until death do us part." Since neither of us are dead, we're not parting. I guess I looked back over the years and how you had behaved toward certain people, and the puzzle pieces began to fit. It was remarkable. The Lord had it all worked out for us in coming here.

Q. *Tell how you viewed our relationship during the most troubling time of therapy?*

A. Well, we were in it together. The scriptures say you become one flesh. As many years as we've been married, I think we have experienced that. How many times have I told you that we all bring baggage into a relationship? e don't know because it is hidden. It's out of view and out of the memory. The time was right for us to throw the baggage from the train and not carry it any more. How many times have you said to me, "I'm in a tunnel. I don't think I'll ever see the light of day or see any kind of light." You felt like you were in darkness all the time; all alone, hopeless, and helpless. I kept assuring you that one day we'd come out of this, and you would always ask when. You wanted to be done quickly. You worked so hard at it--persistent, stubborn, and yet not yielding an inch. You always wanted to go forward, and the Lord graciously gave you strength, grace, and help every step of the way. He carried us for a long time. There was only one set of footsteps in the sand. He was carrying us.

When it was so hard and we both knew you had MPD, I would see the behavior of a child. I would come home and instead of having just two boys, I had two boys and a little girl. It is certainly different to see an adult woman's body but watch her act like a child.

I just knew it was all going to work out no matter how hard it got. And it did get hard for all of us. I just had that confidence even though it was very small and weak. Concerning myself, there were times suicide crossed my mind. I wondered if something happened to me, what would happen to our boys? Where would they go; what would they do? It was like a proverbial hard place--between a rock and a hard place. I had nowhere to go, and I did feel all alone. Some of the people with whom I worked knew what was going on. Yet I still felt all alone. It was okay when I was around people--I had something to preoccupy myself, my mind, and my thinking. When I came home and you were in the hospital, the boys were here, but they went to bed at a decent hour. Then I would be alone and that's when it really got bad. I don't hold that against you. It was never your fault. I never held it against you and I never will. You were a victim and you had enough courage and loved yourself enough to seek and find help.

I knew you had had a bad self image for many, many years (*I'm not as old as it sounds*], but you sought help and found it. (*I was driven because of my love for you and our boys.*] I remember quoting scripture to you. Jesus said you are to "love the Lord your God with all your heart, mind, soul and strength" and "your neighbor as yourself." You had a hard time loving your neighbor because you had a hard time loving yourself. In actuality, you do love yourself because you did something about your problem. I am proud of you-I always have been and always will be.

Q. *What was your reaction when you found out I was MPD? Could you tell when I was disassociating? Also thinking back on our first years together, could you tell I was disassociating then?*

A. I didn't think you were strange or weird, but it helped me to see why you behaved like you did. I didn't know a lot about it. I read up on it and talked to people. I began to have a better understanding. The light went on in my head; it all fit. I thought of all these different incidents all through the years--how you had behaved at certain times, in certain places, around certain people. It all fit. You sure didn't like some guys. You would just like to punch their eyes out.

I could tell when you were disassociating. You acted like a little girl. You weren't the adult Glenda. You weren't sure of yourself. You were always worried if someone would love you. If you did something, would they still like you--Gloria, Mrs. Smith, Janet, and even me? It got to be a pattern. I expected it and you didn't disappoint me.

I remember when we were together I talked to Amber, Cindy, and Red. I could tell after awhile to whom I was talking. It was interesting. I was trying to gain their trust and confidence because you'd already been hurt enough by your dad. I never wanted to hurt you. (*He didn't either. He was very gentle.*]

Your work around the house slowly went down hill. As far as your role as a wife, it fell off dramatically. You couldn't cook a meal, do laundry, work. I didn't trust you to drive. You were like a little kid in so many different ways.

Thinking of our first years together, I remember the testing. You would ask, "So you love me?" I didn't think anything about it. I never put two and two together until we found out that you were MPD. I didn't have any knowledge of that back in 1981. I thought that's just how you were and that was fine. You were me wife and I loved you, regardless.

Q. *Did you question my spirituality even though I quit school and stopped going to church?*

A. No, I never questioned your spirituality. You didn't quit school. You had to drop out because you were busy putting your time and energy into working on your emotional being and your memories. You didn't have enough strength later to do the kind of school work you were capable of doing. You gave a heroine's effort those first couple of years--working a job, being a full-time mom, doing church work and going to school. WOW. It's amazing, looking back on it, how you even did it. You did very well. You finally ran out of gas. I'm glad you did.

Stop going to church? You were going to a support group on Sunday nights and you needed that. I was having a hard time, and I wanted to protect you. I didn't want to see you hurt anymore. I was the protector. I had to change roles too. I had to go with the flow. You might have given up on yourself at times or thought, "What's the use? God doesn't love me anymore." I guess if I had had all your memories and what went into your years, not being loved and just being put down so much, I would have questioned also. If God really loved me, why did He allow these things to happen? I don't think anyone who had walked in your shoes would have done it any differently. God never gave up on us even though we might sometimes have given up on Him. He loves us so much. That is why He sent

Jesus to die for us. He then could provide that grace, help, understanding, and mercy for all of us.

Q. *If you could do things over, would you still commit me to the hospital? How were things for you at this time?*

A. Well, you know I told you that was one of the lowest points of my life. I felt like the scum of the earth. Just even thinking about it brings tears to my eyes. I didn't want to do it. I know you have said I had no choice. You forced me to realize that, and I know I had to do it, but I did not like it. If suicide was ever on my mind, it was in those days. I went into a survival mode myself. I tried not to think about it because it hurt so much. You know I had to be strong for the boys--I was both Dad and Mom. I had to get them ready for school, fix their meals and do laundry. I had to function like that for nearly one hundred days. I was Mr. Mom.

The nights were lonely. I couldn't sleep very well; you weren't there beside me. I went to bed really late and didn't get much sleep. It was really hard trying to finish my Master's Degree. The only thing that I can think of is that the Lord helped me every step of the way, even though I didn't realize it sometimes. I didn't sense it a lot of the time or didn't think about it. I was numbed by the situation and in an automatic mode.

I would tell Gloria that my feelings were buried. “I don't need them right now, I can't function with them. They have to be put back.” I'm so thankful we have friends like Gloria and her family. I don't know what we would have done without them. We thought we moved here to work on our Master's Degrees, but as I told one of the professors, we have received more than an academic degree here. He just smiled and shook his head yes.

It was hard when you said you didn't want to see me because you were embarrassed. A friend had come to see you, and you asked her to call me and ask me to come. She called and I was glad to come and see you. The next time I just won't listen to you and will come anyway. Let me back up. I don't think you'll ever have to go back in the hospital in that capacity again. I think you are doing a lot better and are well on the road to recovery. I don't see there is any room for relapse.

It was hard going out to the hospital every week-end. Gloria and her family would take care of the boys and I would go to the hospital. Spending Saturday and Sunday with you, I'd get very tired. I'd tell Gloria I hadn't done anything, but I was tired nevertheless. She said, "That takes a lot out of you.” It finally dawned on me the emotional energy being used. It was a tremendous amount. But I was there every week-end. (*Boy, was I glad.)*

I remember taking you out for a weekend pass. I was so protective of you. I didn't want anything to happen. I didn't even want the boys to raise their voices or anything. Mr. Mean Guy, Mr. Protector. Everything suffered while you were gone. At my work I was not enthusiastic, and people probably complained. I told several people I wouldn't wish this on my worst enemy. It was too hard a struggle, more than a person can imagine.

Q. *How do you view things now, as far as recovery goes?*

A. Remember that December day when I picked you up at the hospital and I put your ring back on your finger? I said our marriage vows over again to you, and I was excited to have you home. You also were happy to be home. It was like having my wife back after about two or three years. Sure, you had a long way to go in recovery, but you were over the worst. I was thrilled and rejoicing.

Now we could have intelligent conversations. It wasn't like just talking to the boys. I can talk to an adult. You function better than you ever have. I know it is hard working through your emotions, because you had pushed them down and suppressed them for so long. You are finding it hard because you are breaking new ground. I know you get frustrated. I'm trying to be patient and understanding.

Even now in August, you weren't worried about me not having employment for awhile. It didn't ruffle you or shake you. You had confidence that I would find a job. Two years ago you would have been a basket case. You've made a lot of progress. I think of how many times I said that you were on the subjective and not seeing clearly. I know there was a time when I went from objective to subjective because I was trying to carry part of your load. So I didn't see so clearly either. There were others around me who were more objective.

I'm more confident now than I've ever been. You are going to do well in school. You will surprise yourself. I really don't know how far along you would be now, if you didn't know Jesus. You still might be in the hospital, or worse. You had that positive, that plus of having a foundation in place in your life. You are farther ahead because of Him. I think that is why you've been able to work through this at the pace you have. I am convinced of that.

God is going to direct you and you're going to help a lot of people. You've been there. You've been down that road. You can say, "I've been there. I know what you're feeling. I know what you're going through." That experience has greater value than any book knowledge could ever have. You can have the book knowledge, but when you have the experience factored in there it is a great combination to help and comfort other people. God is going to use you tremendously. There are many people who have walked the same road you have. They are still looking for someone to help them. You are going to be their help. That is part of God's plan and design for you. I believe that. It will come when the time is right.

You've come a long way, baby, and that's the truth from the horse's mouth.

Chapter 8

FROM THE MOUTHS OF BABES

I don't want to leave my boys out of the picture, because this effected them also. The title of this chapter is not quite true. My boys are not babes. They are young men, so they tell me. I am combining their answers into one. They are twelve and thirteen years old as I write this. Here is how they felt about some events that occurred.

Q. *How did you feel when I was too sick to cook?*

A. I didn't really like it because you couldn't make homemade stuff. If you could sleep all that time, I figured you could at least cook. When I come home from school I'm ready for a good meal.

Q. *How was it when I slept all the time and didn't have time for you?*

A. That really made me mad because I didn't see how someone could sleep so much. You'd sleep for three hours, get up and take a sip of pop, sleep for another three hours, wake up and take another sip of pop, then go to bed. (*I don't think it was quite that bad.*) I thought you should be able to get up and take us someplace. If I slept that much I wouldn’t have had to sleep for two weeks.

Q. *How did you feel when I went to the hospital or while I was there?*

A. The first time I was unsure how to feel. I had mixed feelings. The second time I took it a little better, but the bad thing was that you stayed longer and we couldn't visit you. I was mad because I didn't know what was happening, except that you were getting help. I was sad because you had to go; it was the fact of knowing you were gone.

I was mad because it is fun having you around. You take us places and we didn't get to go anywhere. I was sad because I just didn't want you to go. It stinks like crazy. There was no one around.

It was funny to hear you talk about the meals. We are always telling you how bad the school meals are, and you say they can't be that bad. When you told us about how bad the lunches were at the hospital, I wanted to laugh because it sounded like our school lunches.

Q. *How did you feel about spending so much time at Gloria’s?*

A. It was fun there, but I felt like I was imposing on her because we were there so much. When I was tired I just wanted to be home. I didn't have any of my stuff there, and sometimes I just wanted to be home with my stuff. I didn't get to play with my friends. It was like having a babysitter. I didn't like that. I just wanted to be home.

Q. *How did you feel about going to church without me?*

A. I missed you. I didn't like it that much. I like sitting by you, cause I can talk. I am used to you going to church with us. I cried at church because you were gone. I was thinking about you and just cried.

I didn't care because I knew you were getting help.

Q. *Do you see a difference in me now compared to before I went into the hospital?*

A. Yes. You don't sleep so much. You don't yell at us that much and you let us do more things.

Yes. You seem to like yourself better. You don't sleep as much, you can cook, and take us places. You are more like a mom.

"O My child, lay your heart in My hand, and let me heal it. Yea, let Me gather up thy tears, for they are precious to Me. (Psalms 56:8) Ye have not been suffering alone, but I Myself have been near thee all along the way. My heart has felt all that you have felt. Ye do not have a high priest who is not able to sympathize with your sufferings, but one who experienced every grief and human emotion common to man. And yet, in the midst of these experiences of suffering, He did not sin. Therefore, He is one who is able to succour thee. (Hebrews 2:18)"[5]

If your heart is heavy and you are sure no one understands, then I would challenge you to call on the name of God. He does understand, even when we are not sure what is going on. He is just a whisper away. Stop fighting the battle yourself and call on Him who is able to do above what we can imagine. He sticks closer than a brother. Just give Him a chance. He has most definitely made a big difference in my life. I know He can make a difference in yours.

---

[5]Frances J. Roberts, Come Away My Beloved (Ojai: King's Farspan, Inc., 1970), p. 91.

Epilogue

The actual writing of this book took place in August 1995, at which point I believed I was no longer MPD. This, in fact, was far from the truth. A few months after writing *An Unspeakable Secret,* I began to have trouble again. To my surprise it was another group of alters, which was followed by yet another group. The next five years were as troublesome as the ones I have written about.

As I type this, I am proud to report to all that I am done with therapy and am fully integrated. God gave my family and me the strength and courage to see this long hard journey to completion. Maybe someday I will have the opportunity to share the rest of the story with you as well.

ANNOTATED BIBLIOGRAPHY

Allender, Dr. Dan B. The Wounded Heart. Colorado Springs: Navpress, 1990.

This book not only tells of abuse and the damage it does to people, but it gives a very spiritual look at dealing with the problem. It does not leave one in a hopeless state but in a state of hope, knowing that with God's help one can receive the healing only God can give.

Chase, Truddi. When Rabbit Howls. New York: Jove Books, 1990.

A moving true story of a lady who has multiple personality disorder. She has 92 personalities living within her which she refers to as the Troops.It gives details of the different personalities and how they act, dress and generally conduct themselves. It is a very stirring book to know someone really lives like that day after day.

Courtwright, John & Roger, Dr. Sid. Your Wife Has Been Sexually Abused. Grand Rapids: Zondervan Publishing House, 1994.

An excellent book explaining some of the feelings an abused person experiences. It guides the spouse in how to deal with the situation, giving pointers in what to do or not to do or say. It is very simply written, so the common lay person can easily understand and grasp the facts stated.

Friesen, James G. Ph. D. More Than Survivors Conversations With Multiples. San Bernardino: Here's Life Publishers, Inc., 1992.

Questions are asked of the multiples, and they share their true feelings from their heart. They talk about being a multiple and even the hope some have of integrating. Some tell of their experience after being integrated. It was interesting to see that those seeking integration and hose already integrated were not sure if this could be done without the Lord helping them. A book to help see how a multiple thinks.

Gil, Eliana Ph. D. Outgrowing The Pain. New York: Dell Publishing, 1983.

Have you been abused? Do you think you might have been? Read this small book to help you see what has happened and why you react in the varied ways you do. Also find out what to do about that terrifying past.

Ritchie, Bill. A Dad Who Loves You. Sisters: Multnomah Press Books, 1992.

An inspirational book giving a new and fresh look at God the Father. Scriptures are quoted to help you see Jesus as a caring, loving person; a Father you can trust to do what is best for you. An excellent book for anyone having trouble relating to God as Father.

FURTHER READING

Bass, Ellen & Davis, Laura. The Courage to Heal. New York: Harper Perennial, 1988.

Bassoff, Evelyn S. Mothering Ourselves: Help & Healing for Adult Daughters. A Plume Book, 1991.

Bradshaw, John. Bradshaw On: The Family. Deerfield: Health Communications, 1988.

Friesen, James G. Ph. D. Understanding the Mystery of MPD. Nashville: Thomas Nelson Publishers, 1991.

Ney, Philip G. M.D. Ending The Cycle of Abuse. New York: Brunner/Mazel Inc., 1995.

Stapleton Ruth. The Gift of Inner Healing. Waco: Word Books, 1976.